PASTA LIGHT

PASTA LIGHT

80 Low-Fat, Low-Calorie, Fast & Fabulous Pasta Sauces

NORMAN KOLPAS

CB

CONTEMPORARY
BOOKS

CHICAGO

Library of Congress Cataloging-in-Publication Data

Kolpas, Norman
    Pasta light : 80 low-fat, low calorie, fast & fabulous pasta
sauces / Norman Kolpas.
       p.   cm.
    ISBN 0-8092-4177-3 :
    1. Sauces.   2. Cookery (Pasta)   I. Title.
TX819.A1K64   1990
641.8'22—dc20   90-34746
                                         CIP

Published by Contemporary Books, Inc.
Two Prudential Plaza, Chicago, Illinois 60601-6790
Manufactured in the United States of America
International Standard Book Number: 0-8092-4177-3

CONTENTS

ACKNOWLEDGMENTS

I am grateful to the following people who served as taste-testers for the recipes in this book: Alice Bandy; Nicolas Bianco; Martha, Henry, and Morwenna Lytton Cobbold; Hu Goldman; Peter Goldman; Caryn Landau; Evonne and Joseph Magee; Dave McCombs; Lois McKeen; and Susan, Michael, and Andrew Rubin.

As always, my wife, Katie, was the most enthusiastic, critically keen, and supportive tester of them all, making sure that she had at least a bite of every single recipe in this book. And our new son, Jacob, though not yet old enough to tuck into a plate of pasta, showed remarkable perseverance and high spirits during the entire ordeal of testing. This book is as much theirs as it is mine.

Other thanks are due as well. I'd be remiss if I didn't thank my doctor, Paul Geller, M.D., who planted one of the first seeds for this book when he told me that he'd begun adapting some of the recipes in my earlier sauces book, *Pasta Presto*, to his own dietary needs. And special thanks go to my editor, Nancy Crossman, and everyone at Contemporary Books for the fine, professional, creative, and warm-hearted way they all go about the business of publishing.

PASTA LIGHT

INTRODUCTION

"I *love* pasta. If only it weren't so fattening!"

That's a common lament heard from people who love to cook and eat. And what most people still don't realize is that pasta itself isn't fattening—just 190 calories or so in a 1-cup serving of spaghetti cooked *al dente* (slightly chewy), for example. And that same cup has less than 1 gram of fat, no cholesterol at all, and only about 1 milligram of sodium.

A pretty good little dietary package, all in all. But what loads the calories, fat, and salt onto that pristine cup of pasta are the sauces—all the butter, cream, oil, and cheese with which we're used to bathing our pasta before it ever enters our mouths.

I heard a lot of laments from calorie- and fat-conscious pasta lovers after I published my first book of sauces, *Pasta Presto*. While many of the recipes in that book are very healthy and fairly low in calories—and all of them, so people who have cooked from it tell me, work well and taste good—there are a fair number of recipes that revel in fairly sinful ingredients. Wasn't there some way, friends and acquaintances would ask me, to enjoy a wider range of pasta sauces that were still good for you?

The book you now hold in your hands is a positive answer to that question. *Pasta Light* offers a healthy alternative for diet-conscious pasta lovers—more than

80 recipes for fresh, delicious sauces that are low in calories, fat, cholesterol, and sodium.

In fact, *anyone* who enjoys good food should find the recipes on the following pages tasty and satisfying. I've achieved that end by applying some basic principles of cooking and sauce making to the development of these recipes. Most important of all is the principle of reduction—the fact that by simmering or boiling a liquid for a prolonged period of time you concentrate its flavor. Many of the recipes in this book get a flavor boost from concentrated broths or from other liquids that have been long-simmered. I've also tried to enhance the flavors of these sauces with the many fresh and dried herbs and spices that are available to the modern cook.

In addition, I've taken great advantage of the wide range of diet-conscious products that you'll find on the shelves of supermarkets everywhere today—from cholesterol-free oils to natural egg substitutes, light-style cheeses to creamy-tasting evaporated nonfat milk, salt-free canned tomatoes to produce, meats, poultry, and seafood of such exemplary quality and freshness that their flavors and textures almost sparkle.

On the next few pages, you'll find a guide to the ingredients used in this book, along with recipes and instructions for basic preparations, and other advice useful to the cooking and enjoyment of light pasta. The sauce recipes that follow this introductory section are divided into four chapters based on their predominant ingredients: vegetables; seafood; poultry and meat; and dairy products.

I've aimed to offer a widely varied selection of recipes, to suit your every taste and craving. More important, I hope you'll find all these recipes an inspiration—an idea of what it's possible to achieve when you set out to make healthy, delicious food. As you prepare these recipes and grow more familiar with them and the principles behind them, please feel free to start adapting and playing with them in your own kitchen to come up with your own versions of light pasta sauces.

AN IMPORTANT NOTE ON DIETARY INFORMATION AND SPECIAL DIETS

As you'll see while flipping through the pages of this book, every recipe includes information on the amount of calories, fat, cholesterol, and sodium per serving.

But this is not intended to be a diet book. While the recipes may well help you pursue your own dietary goals, your only source for dietary guidance must and should be your personal physician. Please be sure to check with him or her before you embark on any regimen that involves limiting your calories, fat, cholesterol, sodium, or any other dietary factors.

That said, these recipes do fall well within established guidelines for healthy eating. The American Heart Association, for example, recommends that members of the general population should get no more than about 30 percent of their calories from fat. For a moderately active, 160-pound man—who needs 2,400 calories a day to maintain his weight—that works out to 800 calories from fat, which is the equivalent of a little less than 89 grams of dietary fat per day (1 gram of fat yields 9 calories). Flipping through the recipes, you'll see that the vast majority of sauces have well below 10 grams of fat per serving, with none higher than about 15 grams and many as low as 3 grams or less—all falling well within these guidelines for anyone pursuing a healthy diet.

Likewise, the American Heart Association now recommends that members of the general population eat no more than 100 milligrams of cholesterol per 1,000 calories consumed each day—in other words, 240 milligrams of cholesterol for the 160-pound man we've already referred to. You'll find that many of the recipes in this book contain no cholesterol at all; a rich dairy sauce like Roquefort Cream (see Index) still tops out at just 45 milligrams per serving; and even recipes that include a fairly high-cholesterol ingredient like shrimp are still well below the limit at 129 milligrams.

Those who wish to limit their sodium intake will find these recipes equally accommodating. According to the National Research Council, the recommended daily allowance (RDA) for sodium is between 1,100 and 3,300 milligrams per day. Sodium levels per serving for most of the recipes in this book are well in the low hundreds. I have purposely kept table salt out of the ingredients lists for all the recipes and have aimed to make each recipe taste well seasoned without need of extra salt; but if you aren't watching your salt intake, and wish to add a little extra to your serving, by all means do so.

As for calories, anyone who has ever been at all calorie-conscious will recognize that the counts for the recipes on the following pages, when added to a cup of cooked pasta, which has about 190 calories, result in satisfying dinner-time main courses of well below 500 calories—and in some cases lower than 300 calories—per serving.

It must be noted, though, that the numbers given in each recipe for dietary factors are of necessity approximate. No two identical-looking carrots, onions, pieces of salmon, chicken breasts, portions of cheese—or any other ingredients—will contain exactly the same levels of these or any other dietary or nutritional factors.

Furthermore, while I've strived to use the most widely available, most common ingredients possible, certain canned or packaged goods may not be available everywhere; therefore, the brand of canned light chicken broth, tomatoes, or light-style cheese that you buy in your local market may be higher or lower in calories, fat, cholesterol, or sodium than those with which I developed and tested these recipes.

Throughout this book, then, I have based the dietary readings on average examples of each ingredient in question. The numbers have been derived from government tables and from manufacturers' product information. Use them as general guidelines in your selection of recipes to suit your own particular dietary requirements.

A GUIDE TO BASIC AND SPECIAL INGREDIENTS

Throughout the development and testing of the recipes in this book, I have diligently tried—and, I hope, succeeded—to ensure that the ingredients used are widely available in most supermarkets. In the main, my goal has been to make these recipes with ingredients that are in no way intended for special diets; rather, I've aimed to select ingredients that are inherently good for you, as well as good-tasting, and to combine them for optimum flavor and texture.

In recent years, though, a growing health consciousness among the American public has led to the development of new products that—while not strictly intended for special diets—do take into account the ever-more-widespread interest in controlling calories and in reducing the amount of fat, cholesterol, and sodium in our diets. I've made judicious use of such products, and you'll find them discussed here along with the other ingredients.

But before I review the ingredients, let me leave you with one important piece of advice: Be an active, involved shopper. If you don't find the ingredients you need in your local market, speak to the manager; tell him or her about the product and why you and other customers might like to have it available, and ask that it be ordered for you. A good supermarket manager will always be on the lookout for new products that might appeal to customers and give the market an edge over its competitors. To help you give the manager all the information that might be needed, I've included brand names, along with addresses, for a number of products that still might be difficult to locate in some areas.

Broths and Stocks

To enhance the flavor of many of the recipes in this book, I have included concentrated chicken broth as an ingredient. A number of companies produce salt-free or low-salt broths that you'll find on your supermarket shelves. I performed satisfactory tests with four different brands, all found in one of my local markets: Swanson Natural Goodness, a reduced-salt, clear chicken broth from the Campbell Soup Company, Camden NJ 08103-1701; Campbell's Low Sodium Chicken Broth Soup, from the same source; Health Valley 100% Natural Chicken Broth, a product with no salt added, distributed by Health Valley Foods, Inc., 16100 Foothill Boulevard, Irwindale, CA 91706; and Pritikin Defatted Chicken Broth, a reduced-salt product, from Thompson Kitchens Inc., Springfield, IL 62703. For the bulk of my testing, I used the Swanson product.

To make reduced chicken broth: Put the canned broth of your choice in a heavy saucepan and boil briskly until it has reduced to half of its original volume; in my tests, it took approximately 15 minutes to reduce 2 cups of broth to 1 cup. You may want to stop once or twice and pour the broth into a heatproof measuring cup to check your progress. If you like, reduce the broth in larger quantities and store it in freezer containers; or place it in an airtight container in the refrigerator, where it will keep for several days.

In Chapter 2, "Seafood Sauces," I've also called for rich salt-free fish stock. Fish stock is not as widely available as chicken broth; most canned versions seem to be more seasoned and salted soups than basic cooking ingredients. But I have found that many good fishmongers have fish stock on hand for their customers—either frozen or in some packaged form. You might also want to look for a relatively new product I found in the freezer case of my local market—a "rich fish stock (fumet)" from a company called Perfect Addition, P.O. Box 8976, Newport Beach, CA 92658; they also market frozen poultry and meat stocks.

Cheeses

Laden as it is with butterfat, salt, and calories, cheese may seem to be the complete antithesis of "light." But, knowing that the American public would be hard-pressed to give up one of its favorite foods, enterprising manufacturers have developed a wide range of low-salt, low-fat, low-cholesterol cheeses made from skim or part-skim milk. Among the brands I used in my testing and found to give good results are cheeses sold under the following labels: Dorman's, distributed by Dorman-Roth Foods, Moonachie, NJ 07074; Friendship, from Friendship Dairies, Inc., Friendship, NY 14739; and Lifeline, distributed by Lifeline Food Co., Inc., Seaside, CA 93955.

I did not test, or consider using, the growing number of artificial cheeses based on tofu (soybean curd). For the most part, I have found them to lack the flavor and the cooking properties of real dairy cheese.

And there is one cheese that I've continued to use in its unadulterated form: Parmesan. Sharp and tangy, it generally plays the role of a seasoning rather than a main ingredient in the recipes that follow, and in this way it adds considerable flavor to some recipes at, in my opinion, a minor expense in terms of extra fat and sodium. In most recipes where I've used it, though, please feel free to eliminate it if you want to cut down on those dietary factors.

Egg Substitutes

Among the greatest food developments in recent years for people who are watching their cholesterol are egg substitutes based on real eggs, from which much of the fat and all of the cholesterol have been removed. Sold frozen, these products, when defrosted, can be used just like real beaten eggs, and I've employed them in some of my light versions of dairy sauces that traditionally call for egg. The two best-known brands are available nationwide: Fleischmann's Egg Beaters and Morningstar Farms' Scramblers.

Garlic

Again and again, you'll find garlic seasoning the recipes in this book. In most cases, I use it with subtlety to enhance the flavor of a sauce; in a few cases, I allow garlic to play a more dominant part in a recipe's flavor.

It's a good idea to have a supply of garlic on hand at all times. Buy whole heads and store them in a dry, airy place, where they'll keep well for many weeks or even months. To peel a clove easily, separate it from the head and place it on a work surface. Place the side of a broad-bladed knife on top and hit down carefully and firmly—but not too hard—to crush the clove slightly. The skin will then slip off, leaving the garlic clove ready for chopping.

Powdered garlic and garlic salt are not acceptable as substitutes.

Ham

A number of recipes call for light-style ham. In fact, ham is a relatively lean meat to begin with, but a number of companies offer prepackaged or deli hams that are even lower in fat and that have less salt than conventional hams. Among the many brand names you might look or ask for are: Armour Lower Salt, Boar's Head Lower Salt, Eckrich Calorie Watcher, Light & Lean, and Realean.

Herbs and Spices

A wide range of dried herbs and spices are called for in these recipes. All of them are commonly available in supermarket seasoning sections. Keep them in airtight jars, stored away from light in a cool, dry place.

Many of these recipes also rely on fresh herbs, particularly Italian parsley and basil. Italian parsley, a variety with broad, flat leaves, has an intense flavor beside which that of ordinary crinkly parsley pales to insignificance; by all means seek it out! Fresh basil has become so popular in recent years that it's now virtually a standard item in good supermarket produce sections. If you can't find it, check with your local garden nursery; they can probably sell you basil plants, which thrive in window boxes or gardens.

The same advice holds true for other fresh herbs. If you're serious about light cooking, a kitchen herb garden can be one of your best resources for fresh-tasting, flavorful meals. But, fortunately, there is a growing trend toward using fresh herbs in America's kitchens, and many supermarkets are catering to it by offering an ever-greater variety of these herbs to customers. If you don't see the fresh herb you need, ask the produce manager to order it for you.

Milk

One of the best products I've found to give richness to light pasta sauces is evaporated skim milk—a very-low-butterfat version of the traditional baking and dessert-making product. It's becoming increasingly available in supermarkets. Two national, well-known brands are Pet and Carnation.

Olive Oil

I've tried throughout this book to keep fats and oils to a bare minimum. But in many cases you do need a little oil to brown foods properly. My favorite oil for this purpose is olive oil, which has a rich, fruity flavor that lends its own distinctive character to pasta sauces. And fortunately, olive oil is a monounsaturated oil, a type that not only contains no cholesterol but may even play a small role in lowering the blood cholesterol of people who use it regularly.

Choose only olive oils that are explicitly labeled *extra-virgin*, the designation given to oil extracted from the fruit on the first pressing without heat or chemicals. Every week seems to bring a wider variety of good olive oils to supermarket shelves. Upon inspection, you'll see that they vary from pale golden oils, which have very mild flavors, to dark green ones in which the true taste of the olive comes through. While darker oils are more to my taste, feel free to taste, compare, and select an olive oil that is right for you.

Store your olive oil in its airtight container, away from light and heat.

Olives

In a few recipes in this book, I call for low-salt canned black olives. The brand I used, called Lindsay, contains one-third less salt than conventional canned black olives. It is distributed by Lindsay International, Inc., Lindsay, CA 93247.

Sugar

In many of the recipes that call for canned tomatoes, and even in those using fresh ones, you'll see that I've also added a little sugar to enhance the tomatoes' natural sweetness. The sugar adds very few calories and has a wonderful effect on the finished product. But if your own dietary requirements exclude sugar, by all means leave it out of the recipe.

Tomato Concentrate and Paste

A spoonful or two of these ingredients gives a wonderful boost to the flavor of a pasta sauce. The best flavor of all, I've found, comes from imported Italian double-strength tomato concentrate, which is twice as strong as conventional canned tomato paste. It is usually sold in 4.5-ounce tubes and is now widely available. (I use a brand called Amore, imported by Liberty-Richter, Inc., Carlstadt, NJ 07072.) If you can't find the concentrate, substitute twice the amount of canned tomato paste.

Tomatoes

In the summer, it is possible to find good, vine-ripened tomatoes that have an intense tomato flavor. At other times of the year, canned tomatoes are your wisest choice for sauces; and unlike most canned vegetables, canned tomatoes are excellent. Unfortunately, most brands of canned tomatoes for sale on supermarket shelves are loaded with salt. If salt is not a concern for you, by all means use them. But a few manufacturers are now making available canned tomatoes to which no salt has been added. I tested the recipes for this book with a brand of peeled whole canned tomatoes called Nutradiet, distributed by S&W Fine Foods, Inc., San Ramon, CA 94583-1338.

BASIC PREPARATIONS

The following basic preparations are called for and cross-referenced in many recipes in this book:

Peeled and Seeded Tomatoes

Sometimes, the fineness of a sauce requires the removal of the shiny skins and watery, tasteless seed sacs from tomatoes. To peel fresh tomatoes, first bring a large saucepan of water to a boil. With a small, sharp knife, remove the core of each tomato and lightly score its skin into four segments. Carefully put the tomatoes into the water and parboil for 30 to 45 seconds; then lift them out with a slotted spoon. When the tomatoes are cool enough to handle, peel off their skins.

To seed the tomatoes, cut them in half horizontally. With your finger or the handle of a teaspoon, gently scoop out the seeds and discard them.

Roasted Bell Peppers

When roasted, bell peppers develop an intense, sweet flavor that really shines in a pasta sauce or topping. To roast peppers, place them in a foil-lined baking sheet in a 500°F oven. Roast until their skins are evenly blistered and browned, about 25 minutes, turning them two or three times so they roast evenly. Remove them from the oven and cover them with a kitchen towel.

When the peppers are cool enough to handle, pull out their stems; peel away their blackened skins; open the peppers up; and remove their seeds, using a teaspoon to pick up any stray ones.

Take care not to lose any of the peppers' juices, which are also very flavorful. You might want to pour them through a fine-mesh strainer to remove any seeds or bits of skin.

Toasted Pine Nuts

Pine nuts, also known as *pignoli* and *piñónes*, are used to thicken some of the pesto sauces in this book, and in a few cases they are also used as flavorful garnishes to sauces. Toasting them develops and deepens their slightly resinous, nutty flavor. To toast pine nuts, spread them on a foil-lined baking sheet. Place the sheet in a 450°F oven and keep a close eye on the pine nuts, removing them the instant they have turned evenly golden, 5 to 10 minutes.

A SHORT GUIDE TO PASTA

If you're deliberately following a light eating plan, your best choice in pasta is to stick to the most basic dried kind, made from a dough of durum-wheat semolina, which contains no trace of fat, cholesterol, or sodium. Other types of pasta—particularly the freshly made varieties that are so widely available and so appealing in their range of colors, flavors, and shapes—tend to contain eggs and salt and may therefore be taboo on your regimen.

But sticking to one kind of pasta *dough* doesn't mean that you have to limit the variety of pastas you can eat. Over the centuries, ingenious Italian cooks have conjured up literally hundreds of different kinds of pasta shapes and sizes beyond the basic spaghetti, linguine, fettuccine, and macaroni. Many of these are available in good-sized supermarkets, and it's worth seeking out your nearest Italian market or deli to increase your range of choices.

In the introductory note to each sauce recipe, rather than suggesting a laundry list of specific pastas for which it is appropriate, I offer some general guidelines for the types of noodles that work best. In all cases, it's a matter of simple logic: Sauces with a lighter taste and texture generally go better with lighter, more delicate strands of pasta. Thicker sauces full of meats or vegetables are usually best suited to broader noodles. And the thickest, chunkiest sauces logically are best partnered by larger pasta shapes or shells.

When you're planning to make a particular recipe, read over its pasta suggestions, and then refer to the following list for help in making a specific pasta selection:

Strands

Angel Hair. Extrafine strands. In Italian, *capelli d'angelo.*

Bavette. A slightly flattened spaghetti, oval in cross section.

Bucatini. Thin, spaghettilike strands with holes through the center.

Fedelini. Very thin spaghetti.

Fusilli. Like a firecracker fuse: thin, squiggly strands.

Perciatelli. About twice as thick as spaghetti, with a hole running through the center.

Spaghetti. The familiar stringlike pasta.

Vermicelli. "Little worms." A very thin spaghetti.

Ribbons

Fettuccine. Ribbons about ¼ inch wide.

Fettuccelli. A narrower form of fettuccine.

Fettucci. Ribbons about ½ inch wide.

Linguine. Very narrow, thick ribbons, like flattened spaghetti.

Mafalde. Wide ribbons with rippled edges.

Papardelle. Wide, short ribbons.

Tagliarini. Small, thin tagliatelli.

Tagliatelli. Similar to fettuccine, but usually somewhat wider.

Shapes

Bocconcini. Grooved tubes about 1½ inches long and ½ inch in diameter.

Bow Ties. Shaped like bow ties. Sizes vary.

Cannolicchi. Small, ridged tubes.

Cavatelli. Narrow shells with a rippled surface.

Conchiglie. Shaped like conch shells, varying in size.

Ditali. Short macaroni tubes.

Farfalle. "Butterflies." Similar to bow ties.

Gemelli. "Twins." Two short strands twisted together.

Gnocchi. Small pasta dumplings.

Macaroni. Refers to any tube pasta, but most often to the familiar *elbow* macaroni—small to medium-sized, short, curved tubes.

Maruzze. Shells, varying from small to very large, sometimes smooth, sometimes ridged.

Mostaccioli. "Little moustaches." Medium-sized tubes, about 2 inches long, with diagonally cut ends. Sometimes smooth, sometimes grooved.

Penne. "Quill pens." Short, narrow tubes with ends cut diagonally like an old-fashioned pen. Sometimes grooved.

Rigatoni. Large, ridged tubes.

Ruote. Wagon-wheel shapes.

Rotelli. Corkscrew shapes.

Ziti. Large, macaronilike tubes cut into short lengths.

COOKING PASTA

For the best results, it's always wisest to follow the manufacturer's instructions on the pasta box, as cooking times will vary depending on how thick and how dry the pasta is. But these guidelines will help you get good results:

- Use a large quantity of water relative to the amount of pasta you are cooking. There should be plenty of room in the pot for the water to circulate freely around the pasta so that the pasta doesn't stick together.
- Common wisdom holds that you should add salt to the pot to help the water boil faster and season the pasta slightly. This isn't necessary.
- Common wisdom also holds that you should add a splash of oil to the water to help keep the pasta from sticking together. While this does help, it isn't absolutely necessary; and if you leave the oil out, you'll wind up with less fat and fewer calories in the final dish.
- To test for doneness, fish out a strand or piece of pasta with a long fork near the end of the cooking time. *Al dente*—cooked through but still chewy—is the preferred way to eat pasta.
- Drain the cooked pasta thoroughly, but do not rinse it. Serve immediately.

PASTA PORTIONS

All of the recipes in this book yield enough sauce for four 1-cup servings of cooked pasta.

A NOTE ON COOKING TIMES

Please note that all cooking times given for the recipes in this book are approximate; I have tried to give a range of cooking times, along with sensory descriptions that should help you judge when something has cooked long enough. Cooking times will vary with the size of the cooking vessels you use, the materials they are made of, the peculiarities of your stove, the altitude at which you live, and your personal approach to cooking. The main principle to bear in mind is that any sauce will reduce far more quickly in a large, wide saucepan than in a smaller, narrower one with less surface area.

In the end, though, the best way of judging when something is ready is to learn to use your sight, hearing, taste, and touch.

Throughout the recipes, I describe sauces that are done cooking as *thick but still slightly liquid*. If you feel at all uncomfortable judging that description, the easiest way I've found to test is by scraping a wooden or plastic spoon along the bottom of the pan or skillet: It should leave a discernible trace that lasts for a second or so before the liquid flows back and covers it up.

1
VEGETABLE SAUCES

FRESH TOMATO WITH FRESH HERBS
UNCOOKED FRESH TOMATOES VINAIGRETTE
MIXED ROASTED PEPPERS VINAIGRETTE
CREAMY TOMATO WITH HOOP CHEESE
ROASTED TOMATO AND RED CHILE ARRABIATA
YELLOW TOMATO SAUTE
GARLIC, PINE NUTS, AND OLIVE OIL WITH FRESH TOMATO
SPICY EGGPLANT WITH TOMATOES
CHUNKY BELL PEPPERS AND TOMATOES
SPICED LENTILS WITH TOMATOES
WHITE BEANS WITH TOMATOES
BLACK OLIVES WITH TOMATOES AND CAPERS

MUSHROOM BOLOGNESE
MIXED MUSHROOM SAUTE
BABY ARTICHOKE HEART SAUTE
ASPARAGUS GREMOLATA
GRILLED BABY VEGETABLES
SPAGHETTI SQUASH WITH HERBS AND PARMESAN
CARROTS AND HAM IN GINGERED CHICKEN BROTH
ZUCCHINI AND GOLDEN SQUASH SAUTE WITH HOOP CHEESE
BROCCOLI WITH SUN-DRIED TOMATOES
BROCCOLI WITH RICOTTA
VEGETABLE SPAGHETTI
PARSLEY AND GARLIC WITH OLIVE OIL
YOGURT PRIMAVERA
PRIMAVERA WITH TOMATOES
SPINACH CHIFFONADE IN CHICKEN BROTH
CREAMY SPINACH PESTO
RED BELL PEPPER AND SUN-DRIED TOMATO PESTO
LIGHT BASIL PESTO

FRESH TOMATO
WITH FRESH HERBS

This quick sauce is ideal for summertime, when fresh tomatoes are at their peak. At any other time, you may want to add a little sugar to enhance the tomatoes' flavor. The fresh herbs that add their character to the sauce are becoming increasingly easy to find in good produce departments and at vegetable stands.

Serve with thin-to-medium ribbons or strands.

> 2 **tablespoons olive oil**
> 2 **medium garlic cloves, chopped fine**
> 1½ **pounds Roma or other firm, ripe tomatoes, cored, halved, seeded (see page 9), and coarsely chopped**
> 2 **tablespoons finely shredded fresh basil leaves**
> 2 **tablespoons finely chopped fresh Italian parsley**
> 2 **teaspoons finely chopped fresh oregano leaves**
> 2 **teaspoons finely chopped fresh marjoram leaves**
> 1 **teaspoon finely chopped fresh rosemary leaves**

In a large skillet, heat the oil over moderate heat. Add the garlic and, as soon as it sizzles, stir in the tomatoes and herbs.

Sauté just until the tomatoes' juices thicken, 7 to 10 minutes. Pour over cooked pasta.

Serves 4

Dietary information per serving (sauce only):
Calories: 92   *Cholesterol:* 0 mg
Fat: 7.3 g   *Sodium:* 12 mg

UNCOOKED FRESH TOMATOES VINAIGRETTE

It's a rustic Italian summertime tradition to top pasta with a simple, uncooked mixture of seasoned tomatoes. Make this sauce when vine-ripened tomatoes are at their peak of quality and availability. If you want to make this sauce at any other time of year, you may have to add a teaspoon or two of sugar to enhance the tomatoes' flavor.

Serve over medium strands or ribbons, or toss with medium shapes.

1¾ pounds firm, vine-ripened tomatoes, peeled, cored, halved, seeded (see page 9), and cut into ½-inch pieces
3 tablespoons olive oil
3 tablespoons lemon juice
1½ tablespoons finely shredded fresh basil leaves
1½ tablespoons chopped fresh Italian parsley
Freshly ground white pepper

In a mixing bowl, stir together the tomatoes, oil, lemon juice, basil, and parsley. Season to taste with white pepper and let the mixture sit at room temperature, covered, for 20 to 30 minutes.

Toss with cooked pasta the moment the pasta has been drained.

Serves 4

Dietary information per serving (sauce only):
Calories: 125 *Cholesterol:* 0 mg
Fat: 10.5 g *Sodium:* 26 mg

MIXED ROASTED PEPPERS VINAIGRETTE

Think of this as a sort of hot pasta salad, great as a luncheon main course or as a side dish for lunch or dinner. While it's at its most colorful if you use four different-colored peppers, you can certainly make it with one, two, or three colors if that is all that's available. Use a good, aged balsamic vinegar to complement the sweet flavor of the roasted peppers; if you can't find one, substitute a good-quality red-wine vinegar.

Serve with medium strands, ribbons, or shapes.

1 medium green bell pepper (about 6 ounces)
1 medium red bell pepper (about 6 ounces)
1 medium yellow bell pepper (about 6 ounces)
1 medium orange bell pepper (about 6 ounces)
2 tablespoons olive oil
2 medium garlic cloves, chopped fine
2 tablespoons balsamic or good-quality red-wine vinegar
1 tablespoon finely shredded fresh basil leaves
1 tablespoon finely chopped fresh Italian parsley

Roast, peel, stem, and seed the peppers (see page 10). Tear them into $\frac{1}{4}$- to $\frac{1}{2}$-inch-wide strips and save their juices. Set aside.

In a large skillet, heat the olive oil with the garlic over moderate heat. When the garlic sizzles, add the pepper strips and their juices. Then stir in the vinegar. As soon as the liquid sizzles, stir in the basil and parsley and spoon the sauce over cooked pasta.

Serves 4

Dietary information per serving (sauce only):
Calories: 82   *Cholesterol:* 0 mg
Fat: 7.2 g   *Sodium:* 3 mg

CREAMY TOMATO WITH HOOP CHEESE

Low-fat hoop cheese lends a creamy quality to this mild but flavorful sauce, suffusing it with chewy bits of curd. If you can't find hoop cheese, or want a somewhat richer version, substitute farmer cheese or part–skim–milk ricotta.

Serve with medium strands or ribbons, or with small-to-medium shapes or tubes.

- **1 tablespoon olive oil**
- **2 medium garlic cloves, chopped fine**
- **2 medium shallots, chopped fine**
- **1 16-ounce can salt-free whole tomatoes**
- **6 ounces hoop cheese**
- **2 teaspoons sugar**
- **½ teaspoon dried basil**
- **½ teaspoon dried oregano**
- **Freshly ground black pepper**

In a large skillet or saucepan, heat the oil with the garlic and shallots over moderate heat. When they sizzle, add the tomatoes, breaking them up with your hands. Crumble in the hoop cheese and stir in the sugar, basil, and oregano.

Simmer until the sauce is thick but still slightly liquid, 7 to 10 minutes. Serve over cooked pasta and season to taste with black pepper.

Serves 4

Dietary information per serving (sauce only):
Calories: 102   *Cholesterol:* 1 mg
Fat: 3.8 g   *Sodium:* 25 mg

ROASTED TOMATO AND RED CHILE ARRABIATA

A traditional Italian salsa arrabiata *is made "rabid" by the addition of crushed red chile flakes. This Southwestern variation gets its fire from a long, red, dried New Mexican chile—the kind frequently sold loose in supermarket produce sections or packaged in clear plastic in the spice aisle. Roasting both the tomatoes and the chile intensifies their flavors and produces a sensational brick-red sauce that can also be used as a background for grilled chicken or meat.*

Whenever you handle hot chiles, avoid touching your eyes or any cuts or abrasions, and be sure to wash your hands thoroughly with soap and water afterwards.

Serve over thin-to-medium strands or ribbons.

> **2 pounds large, firm, ripe tomatoes**
> **1 large, long, red, dried New Mexican chile (about 1½ ounces)**
> **1 tablespoon olive oil**
> **2 medium garlic cloves, chopped fine**
> **1 teaspoon sugar**
> **1 teaspoon dried oregano**
> **1½ tablespoons chopped fresh cilantro leaves**

Preheat the oven to 500°F. With a fork, pierce the tomatoes near their stem ends. Put them in a baking pan lined with aluminum foil. Put the chile in a separate foil-lined pan. Put both pans in the oven.

Roast the chile until it turns evenly dark brown, 5 to 7 minutes. Remove it from the oven and set it aside. Continue roasting the tomatoes until their skins are evenly blackened, about 45 minutes.

With your hands, split open the chile and remove its stem and seeds. Break its flesh and skin into a food processor fitted with the metal blade. Pulse the machine on and off several times until the chile is finely chopped.

Add the tomatoes to the processor, including their skins and any juices that have collected in the pan. Pulse the machine until the tomatoes are chopped to a coarse puree.

In a large saucepan or skillet, heat the oil with the garlic over moderate heat. When the garlic begins to brown, add the tomato-chile mixture and stir in the sugar and oregano. Simmer until thick but still slightly liquid, about 5 minutes.

Stir in the cilantro and serve over cooked pasta.

Serves 4

Dietary information per serving (sauce only):
Calories: 76	*Cholesterol:* 0 mg
Fat: 3.9 g	*Sodium:* 16 mg

YELLOW TOMATO SAUTE

Thanks to enterprising growers, every day seems to bring more variety to the produce department. A case in point is yellow tomatoes—actually bright golden orange varieties that pop up at my local market with ever-increasing frequency and seem to me to taste even sweeter than vine-ripened red tomatoes. Taste aside, their vibrant color alone makes them a spectacular pasta topping.

Serve with medium strands, ribbons, shapes, or shells.

- **2 tablespoons olive oil**
- **2 medium garlic cloves, chopped fine**
- **1½ pounds yellow tomatoes, stemmed, cored, and chopped into ½- to 1-inch pieces**
- **2 tablespoons finely shredded fresh basil leaves**
- **2 tablespoons finely chopped fresh Italian parsley**
- **1 teaspoon sugar**
- **Freshly ground black pepper**

In a large skillet, heat the olive oil with the garlic over moderate heat. When the garlic begins to turn golden, after 1 to 2 minutes, add the tomatoes and stir in the herbs and sugar.

Simmer, stirring frequently, until the sauce is thick but still somewhat liquid, 5 to 7 minutes. Pour over cooked pasta and season to taste with black pepper.

Serves 4

Dietary information per serving (sauce only):
Calories: 94   *Cholesterol:* 0 mg
Fat: 7.1 g   *Sodium:* 12 mg

GARLIC, PINE NUTS, AND OLIVE OIL WITH FRESH TOMATO

This is a beautiful summertime pasta dish, quick to make and full of vivid flavors and colors.

Serve over thin-to-medium strands or ribbons.

- ¼ **cup olive oil**
- ¼ **cup pine nuts**
- 4 **medium garlic cloves, chopped fine**
- ¼ **cup reduced chicken broth (see page 6)**
- ½ **pound tomatoes, peeled, cored, halved, seeded (see page 9), and cut into ¼-inch dice**
- ¼ **cup finely chopped fresh Italian parsley**

In a large skillet, heat the olive oil with the pine nuts and garlic over moderate heat. As soon as the pine nuts turn golden, after about 2 minutes, pour in the broth, taking care to avoid splattering. As soon as it simmers, pour the sauce over cooked pasta. Garnish with tomato and parsley.

Serves 4

Dietary information per serving (sauce only):
Calories: 187   *Cholesterol:* 0 mg
Fat: 18.9 g   *Sodium:* 93 mg

SPICY EGGPLANT WITH TOMATOES

Try to make this with long, slender Japanese eggplants, if your store carries them. They tend to have fewer seeds than standard-size eggplants and, being smaller, will make it easier for you to buy exactly the amount you need. If you want the sauce even spicier, feel free to increase the red pepper flakes; ¼ teaspoon more will make it fairly fiery.

Serve with medium-to-large ribbons or shapes.

> **3 tablespoons olive oil**
> **2 medium garlic cloves, chopped fine**
> **½ teaspoon crushed red pepper flakes**
> **½ pound eggplant, peel left on, cut into ½- to 1-inch chunks**
> **1 16-ounce can salt-free whole tomatoes**
> **½ tablespoon dried basil**
> **½ tablespoon dried oregano**
> **1 bay leaf**

In a large skillet or saucepan, heat the olive oil with the garlic and pepper flakes over moderate heat. When the garlic sizzles, reduce the heat to low, add the eggplant, and sauté until it begins to soften and the garlic begins to turn brown, 2 to 3 minutes.

Add the tomatoes, breaking them up with your hands, and stir in the remaining ingredients. Cover and simmer gently until the eggplant is tender and the sauce is thick, 15 to 20 minutes.

With a wooden spoon, gently press on the pieces of eggplant to mash them slightly into the sauce. Serve over cooked pasta.

Serves 4

Dietary information per serving (sauce only):
Calories: 143   *Cholesterol:* 0 mg
Fat: 10.3 g   *Sodium:* 22 mg

CHUNKY BELL PEPPERS AND TOMATOES

This robust, colorful sauce takes advantage of the growing variety of bell peppers available in our markets today. Feel free to use whatever—and however many—kinds are available to you.

Serve with medium strands, ribbons, or shapes.

- **2 tablespoons olive oil**
- **2 medium garlic cloves, chopped fine**
- **1 small green bell pepper (about 5 ounces), halved, seeded, and cut into ¾- to 1-inch chunks**
- **1 small red bell pepper (about 5 ounces), halved, seeded, and cut into ¾- to 1-inch chunks**
- **1 small yellow bell pepper (about 5 ounces), halved, seeded, and cut into ¾- to 1-inch chunks**
- **1 16-ounce can salt-free whole tomatoes**
- **1 tablespoon double-concentrate tomato paste**
- **1 tablespoon finely shredded fresh basil leaves**
- **2 teaspoons dried oregano**
- **½ tablespoon lemon juice**

In a large skillet or saucepan, heat the oil with the garlic over moderate-to-high heat. As soon as the garlic begins to sizzle, add the peppers and sauté, stirring constantly, until they are tender, 7 to 10 minutes.

Reduce the heat to moderate-to-low and add the tomatoes, breaking them up with your hands. Stir in the remaining ingredients and simmer until thick but still slightly liquid, 7 to 10 minutes. Serve over cooked pasta.

Serves 4

Dietary information per serving (sauce only):
Calories: 117   *Cholesterol:* 0 mg
Fat: 7.1 g   *Sodium:* 61 mg

SPICED LENTILS
WITH TOMATOES

In India, this might be called a dal—*the name affixed to most dishes that feature lentils—and it is an excellent source of protein, dietary fiber, and robust flavor. The lentils are seasoned here with a blend of common Indian spices, all of which are available in most supermarket spice sections.*

Serve over medium strands or ribbons, or with medium-sized shapes or tubes.

> **1 tablespoon corn or peanut oil**
> **3 medium garlic cloves, chopped fine**
> **1 small onion, chopped fine**
> **1 teaspoon ground cumin**
> **1 teaspoon ground coriander**
> **1 teaspoon powdered ginger**
> **½ teaspoon crushed red pepper flakes**
> **1 16-ounce can salt-free whole tomatoes**
> **1 cup reduced chicken broth (see page 6)**
> **½ cup brown lentils**
> **1 tablespoon sugar**
> **½ cup low-fat yogurt**
> **2 tablespoons finely shredded fresh basil leaves**

In a large skillet or saucepan, heat the oil with the garlic and onion over moderate heat. When they sizzle, add the cumin, coriander, ginger, and red pepper flakes and sauté for 1 minute more.

Add the tomatoes, breaking them up with your hands, and stir in the broth, lentils, and sugar. Simmer until the lentils are tender and the sauce is thick, about 30 minutes. Then stir in the yogurt and the basil and spoon over cooked pasta.

Serves 4

Dietary information per serving (sauce only):
Calories: 198   *Cholesterol:* 1 mg
Fat: 5.2 g   *Sodium:* 399 mg

WHITE BEANS WITH TOMATOES

Robust and filling, this sauce recalls rustic home-style Italian cooking.
Serve over medium-to-wide strands, ribbons, tubes, or shapes.

1 tablespoon olive oil
2 medium garlic cloves, chopped fine
1 small onion, chopped fine
2 ounces thinly sliced light-style ham, cut into ¼-by-
    1-inch strips
¼ cup reduced chicken broth (see page 6)
1 16-ounce can salt-free whole tomatoes
1 cup canned Italian white beans (cannellini),
    thoroughly rinsed and drained
1 tablespoon double-concentrate tomato paste
1 tablespoon finely chopped fresh savory leaves
1 tablespoon finely shredded fresh basil leaves
1 tablespoon finely chopped fresh Italian parsley
2 teaspoons sugar
1 teaspoon dried oregano

In a large skillet or saucepan, heat the oil with the garlic, onion, and ham over moderate-to-high heat. When they begin to brown, after 3 to 5 minutes, add the broth, stirring and scraping to deglaze. Then add the tomatoes, breaking them up with your hands, and stir in the remaining ingredients.

Simmer the sauce until it is thick but still slightly liquid, about 15 minutes. Spoon over cooked pasta.

Serves 4

Dietary information per serving (sauce only):
Calories: 146   *Cholesterol:* 6 mg
Fat: 4.1 g   *Sodium:* 367 mg

BLACK OLIVES WITH TOMATOES AND CAPERS

Most of us tend to think of olives as a salty, fatty food. But it's possible to buy low-salt black olives—featured in this Mediterranean-style sauce—that have all of the good flavor without all of the salt. Yes, the capers that lend spark to the sauce are themselves salty; but you can cut down on their saltiness by choosing a brand that ranks salt further down—and thus in lesser concentration—on the ingredients list, and then draining and rinsing the capers well before adding them.

Serve with medium-to-large strands, ribbons, or shapes.

1 tablespoon olive oil
3 medium garlic cloves, chopped fine
1 small (3-ounce) onion, coarsely chopped
1 16-ounce can salt-free whole tomatoes
1 cup (about 48) medium-sized canned, low-salt,
    pitted black olives, drained and broken by hand or
    chopped into about 4 pieces each
3 tablespoons capers, drained and rinsed
1 tablespoon balsamic or good-quality red-wine
    vinegar
1 tablespoon double-concentrate tomato paste
2 teaspoons sugar
½ tablespoon dried oregano

In a large skillet or saucepan, heat the olive oil with the garlic and onion over moderate heat. When they sizzle, add the tomatoes, breaking them up with your hands. Then stir in the remaining ingredients.

Simmer the sauce until it is thick but still slightly liquid, 5 to 7 minutes. Serve over cooked pasta.

Serves 4

Dietary information per serving (sauce only):
Calories: 140   *Cholesterol:* 0 mg
Fat: 7 g   *Sodium:* 468 mg

MUSHROOM BOLOGNESE

One of my tasters couldn't believe that there was no meat in this sauce. Two tricks contribute to the rich taste. Most basic is the relatively time-consuming process of reducing the mushrooms to a fairly dry essence, which intensifies their flavor. And adding dried shiitake mushrooms to the mixture makes the meaty illusion go even further; they have an almost steaklike flavor that really "beefs up" the sauce.

Serve over medium strands or ribbons, such as spaghetti, tagliatelli, linguine, or fettuccine.

½ ounce dried shiitake mushrooms
½ pound button mushrooms
1 tablespoon olive oil
1 medium shallot, chopped fine
1 medium garlic clove, chopped fine
1 16-ounce can salt-free whole tomatoes
1 tablespoon double-concentrate tomato paste
2 teaspoons sugar
½ tablespoon dried oregano
½ tablespoon dried basil

Put the shiitake mushrooms in a small bowl and add enough warm water to cover. Leave them to soak for about 15 minutes, until soft.

Put the shiitakes and the button mushrooms in a food processor that has been fitted with the metal blade. Process until finely chopped.

In a large skillet, heat the olive oil over moderate heat. Add the shallot and garlic and sauté until tender, 2 to 3 minutes. Add the chopped mushrooms and sauté, stirring frequently, until all the liquid from the mushrooms has evaporated and they have just begun to brown, 10 to 15 minutes.

Add the tomatoes, breaking them up with your hands. Stir in the tomato paste, sugar, oregano, and basil. Simmer until the sauce is thick but still slightly liquid, 10 to 15 minutes. Pour over cooked pasta.

Serves 4

Dietary information per serving (sauce only):
Calories: 105   *Cholesterol:* 0 mg
Fat: 4 g   *Sodium:* 63 mg

MIXED MUSHROOM SAUTE

When sautéed, mushrooms develop an intensity of rich flavor that belies how low in fat and calories they actually are. This quick, simple preparation takes advantage of the ever-increasing variety of fresh mushrooms to be found in supermarkets and produce shops.

In addition to common white or "button" mushrooms, my own two local markets often carry meaty Japanese shiitakes; pale, delicate oyster mushrooms; fragile-looking, dark tree ears; elegant, trumpet-shaped golden chanterelles; and other occasional surprises. I use four kinds of mushrooms in this version. Feel free to vary the recipe depending on what you like and what is available; it's even worth making if all you can find are fresh button mushrooms.

Serve over delicate-to-medium strands or ribbons.

3 tablespoons olive oil

3 medium garlic cloves, chopped fine

2 medium shallots, chopped fine

2 ounces medium-sized fresh button mushrooms, wiped clean with a damp cloth or paper towels, then cut into ¼-inch slices

2 ounces fresh shiitake mushrooms, wiped clean with a damp cloth or paper towels, stems trimmed off, caps cut into ¼-inch slices

2 ounces fresh oyster mushrooms, wiped clean with a damp cloth or paper towels, then cut into ¼-inch slices

2 ounces fresh chanterelle mushrooms, wiped clean with a damp cloth or paper towels, then cut into ¼-inch slices

¼ cup finely chopped fresh Italian parsley

¾ cup reduced chicken broth (see page 6)

1 tablespoon lemon juice

1 ounce grated Parmesan cheese

Freshly ground black pepper

In a large skillet, heat the oil with the garlic and shallots over moderate heat. When they sizzle, raise the heat to high and add all the mushrooms along with the parsley. Sauté, stirring continuously, until the mushrooms just begin to turn golden, 3 to 4 minutes.

Add the broth and lemon juice. As soon as the liquid starts to simmer, pour the sauce over cooked pasta. Sprinkle with Parmesan and season generously with black pepper to taste.

Serves 4

Dietary information per serving (sauce only):
Calories: 149   *Cholesterol:* 5 mg
Fat: 12.5 g   *Sodium:* 357 mg

BABY ARTICHOKE HEART SAUTE

Baby artichokes are among the great pleasures of the produce section—and they're a lot easier to prepare than large ones, since they can be pared in a matter of seconds, and the coarse chokes have yet to develop in their hearts. Rapidly sautéed with a touch of olive oil and a generous amount of garlic, then bathed with some broth and lemon juice, they make a glorious topping for pasta.

Serve with medium pasta strands or ribbons, such as spaghetti, linguine, or fettuccine.

  1 lemon, cut in half
  2 pounds baby artichokes
  2½ tablespoons olive oil
  3 medium garlic cloves, chopped fine
  1¼ cups reduced chicken broth (see page 6)
  3 tablespoons chopped fresh Italian parsley
Freshly ground black pepper

Squeeze and reserve 2½ tablespoons of lemon juice. Fill a mixing bowl with cold water and squeeze the remaining lemon juice into the water.

With a small, sharp knife, stem, pare, and quarter the artichokes, adding them one by one to the bowl of water to keep them from discoloring.

In a large skillet, heat the oil with the garlic over moderate-to-high heat, until the garlic turns a light golden color, 2 to 3 minutes.

Meanwhile, drain the artichokes and pat them dry in a kitchen towel. Add them to the pan and sauté them until they begin to turn golden, 3 to 4 minutes.

Pour in the broth and reserved lemon juice. Bring to a boil, then toss with the parsley. Serve immediately over cooked pasta. Season to taste with black pepper.

Serves 4

Dietary information per serving (sauce only):
Calories: 141   *Cholesterol:* 0 mg
Fat: 10 g   *Sodium:* 506 mg

ASPARAGUS GREMOLATA

When asparagus is abundant, use this simple preparation to highlight its sweet flavor and tender-crisp texture. The Italian garnish known as gremolata *combines orange zest, parsley, and garlic to headily aromatic effect. Use a small, sharp paring knife to cut the strips of zest very carefully from an orange, making sure to remove none of the bitter white pith. Serve over thin-to-medium pasta strands or ribbons, or small pasta shapes.*

12 2-by-½-inch strips orange zest
4 medium garlic cloves
2 tablespoons packed whole Italian parsley leaves
¾ cup reduced chicken broth (see page 6)
¼ cup olive oil
1 pound asparagus, trimmed and cut diagonally
   into ¼-inch slices

Put the orange zest, garlic, and parsley in a food processor fitted with the metal blade. Pulse the machine several times, stopping to scrape down the bowl, then process until finely chopped.

Bring the reduced broth to a boil in a saucepan. Set it aside, covered.

In a large skillet, heat the olive oil over moderate-to-high heat. Sauté the asparagus until tender-crisp, about 3 minutes.

Spoon the asparagus over freshly cooked pasta. Sprinkle with the gremolata, then moisten with the hot broth.

Serves 4

Dietary information per serving (sauce only):
Calories: 145   *Cholesterol:* 0 mg
Fat: 14 g   *Sodium:* 264 mg

GRILLED BABY VEGETABLES

For special entertaining, this dish is nothing short of spectacular—an artful arrangement of quickly grilled baby vegetables arrayed on top of pasta and bathed with chicken broth. You'll find baby vegetables in many well-stocked supermarkets or produce stores nowadays; if your market doesn't carry them, ask the produce department manager before giving up. And if you can't locate them, simply substitute the smallest, freshest "grown-up" vegetables you can find and cut them into thin, decorative slices. Feel free, as well, to alter the assortment you serve, depending on whatever is available and freshest.

The calorie and fat counts, by the way, are lower than you might expect, since about a quarter of the marinade is left behind in the bowl when the vegetables are grilled.

Serve over angel hair or spaghetti.

6 tablespoons olive oil
6 tablespoons freshly squeezed lemon juice
½ teaspoon dried oregano
½ teaspoon dried thyme
½ teaspoon dried marjoram
½ teaspoon dried rosemary
½ pound baby artichokes (about 12), stemmed, pared, and quartered
6 ounces baby zucchini, preferably with blossoms attached, cut in half lengthwise
¼ pound baby acorn squash, cut in half horizontally
¼ pound small Japanese eggplant, trimmed and cut diagonally into ¼-inch-thick slices
¾ cup reduced chicken broth (see page 6)
1 tablespoon chopped fresh Italian parsley
1 tablespoon finely shredded fresh basil leaves
Freshly ground black pepper

Remove the broiler tray and spray it lightly with nonstick coating. Set it aside while you preheat the broiler.

In a large mixing bowl, stir together the olive oil, lemon juice, and herbs. Add the vegetables and toss thoroughly to coat them. Leave the vegetables at room temperature for at least 30 minutes, turning them about every 5 minutes so they marinate evenly.

Place the vegetables on the broiler tray. (Depending on the size of your broiler, it may be necessary to do more than one batch.) Broil close to the heat until golden brown, about 5 minutes per side.

Meanwhile, bring the broth to a boil in a saucepan over low heat; remove from the heat and cover to keep it warm.

Arrange the vegetables on top of cooked pasta and drizzle with the hot broth. Garnish with parsley, basil, and black pepper.

Serves 4

Dietary information per serving (sauce only):
Calories: 177   *Cholesterol:* 0 mg
Fat: 15.8 g   *Sodium:* 278 mg

SPAGHETTI SQUASH WITH HERBS AND PARMESAN

Spaghetti squash is one of the great visual tricks of the vegetable world. Halved and steamed, this gourd yields tender-crunchy, spaghettilike strands that just beg to be tossed with real *spaghetti to make a light-tasting, colorful pasta dish.*

1 3-pound spaghetti squash
2 tablespoons olive oil
2 medium garlic cloves, chopped fine
½ cup reduced chicken broth (see page 6)
½ cup finely chopped fresh Italian parsley
¼ cup finely shredded fresh basil leaves
2 tablespoons lemon juice
1 ounce grated Parmesan cheese
Freshly ground black pepper

With a large, sharp knife, carefully cut the squash in half lengthwise. Use a spoon to scrape out the seeds and their strings from each half.

Put the two halves cut sides down in a large pot (or two pots, if they won't fit in one). Add enough cold water to come 2 inches up the side of the squash. Cover the pot and bring the water to a boil over moderate heat; reduce the heat and simmer until the squash is tender, about 20 minutes.

Drain the squash halves and remove them from the pot. As soon as they are cool enough to handle, use the tines of a fork and lightly scrape out their flesh, which should come out in spaghettilike strands. Discard the shells.

In a large skillet, heat the olive oil with the garlic over moderate heat. As soon as the garlic sizzles, add the spaghetti-squash strands along with the broth, parsley, basil, and lemon juice. Toss gently and, as soon as the liquid simmers, toss the mixture thoroughly with cooked pasta.

Sprinkle with Parmesan and black pepper to taste.

Serves 4

Dietary information per serving (sauce only):
Calories: 148   *Cholesterol:* 5 mg
Fat: 9.3 g   *Sodium:* 301 mg

CARROTS AND HAM IN GINGERED CHICKEN BROTH

There's something about this dish that makes me think of the holiday season, so vivid are its colors and flavors. It's certainly a warming and satisfying sauce for a chilly evening.

Serve over medium strands or ribbons, such as spaghetti, linguine, fettuccine, or fettuccelli.

 2 tablespoons olive oil
 2 medium garlic cloves, chopped fine
 ½ small onion, chopped fine
 2 ounces thinly sliced light-style ham, cut into
   ¼-by-1-inch strips
 1½ cups reduced chicken broth (see page 6)
 ¼ pound carrots, washed, trimmed, and coarsely
   shredded (about 1 cup packed)
 ½ teaspoon finely grated fresh ginger root
 2 tablespoons finely chopped fresh Italian parsley

In a large skillet or saucepan, heat the oil with the garlic and onion over moderate heat. As soon as the vegetables sizzle, add the ham and sauté about 1 minute.

Add the broth, raise the heat, and bring it to a simmer. Then stir in the carrots and ginger. As soon as the broth returns to a boil, stir in the parsley and pour the sauce over cooked pasta.

Serves 4

Dietary information per serving (sauce only):
Calories: 107   *Cholesterol:* 1 mg
Fat: 8 g   *Sodium:* 662 mg

ZUCCHINI AND GOLDEN SQUASH SAUTE WITH HOOP CHEESE

While you can prepare it with regular, green zucchini alone, this fresh-tasting, simple topping will be even more colorful if you make it with a mixture of zucchini and bright yellow, zucchini-shaped golden squash, which is sometimes called yellow or golden squash. Choose fairly small vegetables, no more than about 8 inches long, for the best texture and to avoid seeds.

Zucchini is a watery vegetable, and I had always thought that you had to salt it to draw out its excess liquid. To my surprise, I found that salt isn't entirely necessary; if you simply leave the zucchini shreds to sit briefly, unsalted, you can still squeeze out a fair amount of liquid.

Serve over angel hair, spaghetti, or other thin-to-medium strands.

½ **pound zucchini**
½ **pound golden squash**
3 **tablespoons olive oil**
4 **medium garlic cloves, chopped fine**
1 **cup reduced chicken broth (see page 6)**
2 **tablespoons finely shredded fresh basil leaves**
2 **tablespoons chopped fresh Italian parsley**
2 **teaspoons chopped fresh savory leaves**
¼ **pound hoop cheese**
1 **ounce grated Parmesan cheese**
Freshly ground black pepper

Using a food processor or hand grater, coarsely shred the zucchini and golden squash. Toss the shreds together in a mixing bowl and let them stand for about 10 minutes. Then pick up small handfuls and, working over the sink, squeeze the shreds tightly to extract as much liquid as possible.

In a large skillet, heat the olive oil with the garlic over moderate-to-high heat. As soon as the garlic sizzles, add the shredded vegetables and sauté just until the shreds begin to turn golden, about 4 minutes.

Add the broth, basil, parsley, and savory, stirring well. As soon as the broth simmers, dot rough ½-inch clumps of the hoop cheese all over the surface of the sauce. When the cheese begins to melt, pour the sauce over cooked pasta, sprinkle with Parmesan, and season to taste with black pepper.

Serves 4

Dietary information per serving (sauce only):
Calories: 175   *Cholesterol:* 5 mg
Fat: 13 g   *Sodium:* 440 mg

BROCCOLI WITH
SUN-DRIED TOMATOES

The vibrant contrast of bright green broccoli and brick-red sun-dried tomatoes makes this a beautiful dish. The flavors are equally vivid. Be sure to use sun-dried tomatoes packaged without oil.

Serve with medium-to-wide noodles or medium-sized shells or other shapes.

2	**tablespoons olive oil**
2	**medium garlic cloves, chopped fine**
½	**pound broccoli florets and stems, cut into ½-inch pieces (about 2 cups)**
1	**cup reduced chicken broth (see page 6)**
1	**cup dry white wine**
24	**sun-dried tomatoes, cut with scissors into ¼-inch-wide strips (about 1½ cups)**
1	**teaspoon dried basil**
½	**teaspoon dried oregano**
½	**teaspoon dried thyme**
½	**teaspoon dried marjoram**
	Freshly ground black pepper

Heat the oil in a large saucepan over moderate heat. Add the garlic; as soon as it sizzles, add the broccoli and sauté, stirring continuously, until it turns dark green, about 1 minute.

Add the broth and wine and bring to a boil. Stir in the sun-dried tomatoes and herbs, reduce the heat, cover, and simmer until the broccoli is tender, 10 to 12 minutes.

Spoon over freshly cooked pasta and season with black pepper to taste.

Serves 4

Dietary information per serving (sauce only):
Calories: 218   *Cholesterol:* 0 mg
Fat: 8.4 g   *Sodium:* 390 mg

BROCCOLI WITH RICOTTA

Warming and satisfying, this sauce complements the robust flavor of broccoli with the richness of low-fat ricotta cheese; a sprinkling of caraway seeds adds further interest to the combination. For an even lighter version, you can substitute hoop cheese for the ricotta.

Serve over medium-to-large ribbons, tubes, or shapes.

1 tablespoon olive oil
2 medium garlic cloves, chopped fine
1 small onion, chopped fine
½ tablespoon whole caraway seeds
½ pound broccoli florets and stems, cut into ½-inch pieces (about 2 cups)
1 cup reduced chicken broth (see page 6)
¼ pound part-skim-milk ricotta cheese
2 tablespoons chopped fresh Italian parsley

In a large skillet or saucepan, heat the oil with the garlic, onion, and caraway seeds over moderate heat. As soon as they sizzle, add the broccoli and sauté, stirring continuously, until it turns dark green, about 1 minute.

Add the broth and bring it to a boil. Reduce the heat, cover, and simmer until the broccoli is tender, 10 to 12 minutes.

Dot the sauce with the ricotta and, as soon as it begins to melt, spoon over cooked pasta. Garnish with parsley.

Serves 4

Dietary information per serving (sauce only):
Calories: 109   *Cholesterol:* 10 mg
Fat: 7.2 g   *Sodium:* 382 mg

VEGETABLE SPAGHETTI

Here's a great pasta topping to make when you find yourself with odds and ends of fresh vegetables in the refrigerator. It doesn't use up a single whole vegetable; instead, it combines small quantities of a number of different vegetables in a base of concentrated chicken broth. You can vary the kinds of vegetables used and their proportions to suit your taste and what is available; aim for a total of about ½ pound of vegetables—about 1½ cups of loose shreds—in all, combined in pleasing contrasts of color, flavor, and texture. Be sure to cut the vegetables into the longest shreds you can, using a hand-held grater, so they approximate spaghettilike strands.

Serve this, naturally enough, over spaghetti.

- **2 tablespoons olive oil**
- **2 medium garlic cloves, chopped fine**
- **2 ounces zucchini, shredded (approximately ½ loose cup)**
- **2 ounces golden squash, shredded (approximately ½ loose cup)**
- **2 ounces carrot, shredded (approximately ½ loose cup)**
- **1 ounce celery root, shredded (approximately ¼ loose cup)**
- **1 ounce leek, white part only, shredded (approximately ¼ loose cup)**
- **1 cup reduced chicken broth (see page 6)**
- **1 tablespoon finely shredded fresh basil leaves**
- **1 tablespoon chopped fresh Italian parsley**
- **2 tablespoons grated Parmesan cheese**
- **Freshly ground black pepper**

In a large skillet, heat the olive oil with the garlic over moderate heat. As soon as the garlic sizzles, add the shredded vegetables and sauté, stirring, for about 30 seconds.

Add the broth and bring it to a boil. Simmer briefly, just until the vegetables are tender-crisp. Pour the vegetables and broth over cooked pasta and toss with the basil, parsley, Parmesan, and black pepper to taste.

Serves 4

Dietary information per serving (sauce only):
Calories: 99   *Cholesterol:* 2 mg
Fat: 8 g   *Sodium:* 394 mg

PARSLEY AND GARLIC WITH OLIVE OIL

The most rudimentary of vegetable sauces, this is delicious for a quick, light lunch. Serve over thin-to-medium strands or shapes.

¼ **cup olive oil**
½ **cup finely chopped fresh Italian parsley**
4 medium garlic cloves, chopped fine
¼ **cup reduced chicken broth (see page 6)**

In a large skillet, heat the oil with the parsley and garlic over moderate-to-high heat. When the garlic and parsley sizzle and begin to brown, after 1 to 2 minutes, stir in the broth, taking care to avoid splattering. As soon as it simmers, pour the sauce over cooked pasta.

Serves 4

Dietary information per serving (sauce only):
Calories: 128   *Cholesterol:* 0 mg
Fat: 13.7 g   *Sodium:* 91 mg

YOGURT PRIMAVERA

Primavera or "springtime" sauces, medleys of tender vegetables, usually have tomato or cream bases. While a more conventional tomato primavera follows, this version achieves a light, creamy effect through a combination of reduced chicken broth and low-fat yogurt.

Take the vegetables listed as a very basic guide, to be varied according to your own taste and to what is available.

Serve with medium strands or tubes of pasta, such as spaghetti, tagliatelli, linguine, or penne.

> **1 cup reduced chicken broth (see page 6)**
> **1 tablespoon cornstarch**
> **6 ounces peas in the pod, shelled**
> **2 ounces carrot, cut into ¼-inch dice (approximately ½ loose cup)**
> **2 ounces zucchini, cut into ¼-inch dice (approximately ½ loose cup)**
> **2 ounces golden squash, cut into ¼-inch dice (approximately ½ loose cup)**
> **2 ounces small button mushrooms, cut into ¼-inch slices (approximately ½ loose cup)**
> **1 cup low-fat yogurt**
> **1 ounce grated Parmesan cheese**
> **2 tablespoons chopped fresh Italian parsley**
> **2 tablespoons finely shredded fresh basil leaves**
> **Freshly ground black pepper**

Pour ¼ cup of the broth into a small bowl or cup, and stir in the cornstarch until dissolved. Set aside.

In a medium saucepan, bring the remaining broth to a boil over moderate heat. Add the vegetables and simmer until tender-crisp, about 3 minutes. Stir in the broth-cornstarch mixture, the yogurt, Parmesan, and herbs, and simmer just until thick, 1 to 2 minutes.

Pour the sauce over cooked pasta. Season to taste with black pepper.

Serves 4

Dietary information per serving (sauce only):
Calories: 107   *Cholesterol:* 6 mg
Fat: 3.5 g   *Sodium:* 480 mg

PRIMAVERA WITH TOMATOES

This traditional-style version of the classic Italian springtime vegetable sauce is lightened by the use of salt-free canned tomatoes, and its flavor is enriched with a little reduced chicken broth. Feel free to vary the kinds of vegetables you add according to your taste and what is available.

Serve with medium strands or ribbons, such as spaghetti, linguine, fettuccine, or fettuccelli.

1 tablespoon olive oil

2 medium garlic cloves, chopped fine

2 medium shallots, chopped fine

1 16-ounce can salt-free whole tomatoes

¼ cup reduced chicken broth (see page 6)

1 tablespoon double-concentrate tomato paste

1 teaspoon sugar

1 teaspoon dried oregano

1 bay leaf

2 ounces asparagus, cut into ¼-inch-thick diagonal slices (approximately ½ loose cup)

2 ounces snow peas, cut into ¼-inch-thick diagonal slices

2 ounces carrot, halved lengthwise and cut into ¼-inch-thick diagonal slices (approximately ½ loose cup)

2 ounces golden squash, halved lengthwise and cut into ¼-inch-thick diagonal slices (approximately ½ loose cup)

2 ounces small button mushrooms, cut into ¼-inch slices (approximately ¾ loose cup)

1 tablespoon finely shredded fresh basil leaves

In a large skillet or saucepan, heat the oil with the garlic and shallots over moderate heat. When the vegetables sizzle, add the tomatoes, breaking them up with your hands, and stir in the broth, tomato concentrate, sugar, oregano, and bay leaf.

When the liquid begins to simmer, add the remaining vegetables. Simmer until the sauce is thick but still slightly liquid, about 10 minutes. Stir in the basil and spoon over cooked pasta.

Serves 4

Dietary information per serving (sauce only):
Calories: 96   *Cholesterol:* 0 mg
Fat: 3.7 g   *Sodium:* 149 mg

SPINACH CHIFFONADE IN CHICKEN BROTH

Quick, simple, and colorful, this sauce makes an excellent lunchtime main course.
Serve over medium strands or ribbons such as spaghetti, linguine, or fettuccine.

- **2 tablespoons olive oil**
- **3 medium garlic cloves, chopped fine**
- **4 cups packed raw spinach leaves (from a ¾-pound bunch), stemmed and thoroughly washed, cut into ½-inch-wide strips**
- **2 cups reduced chicken broth (see page 6)**
- **1 ounce grated Parmesan cheese**
- **Freshly ground black pepper**

In a large skillet, heat the olive oil with the garlic over moderate heat. When the garlic sizzles, add the spinach and sauté just until it wilts, about 30 seconds.

Add the broth. As soon as it reaches a simmer, pour the sauce over cooked pasta. Garnish with Parmesan and season to taste with black pepper.

Serves 4

Dietary information per serving (sauce only):
Calories: 113   *Cholesterol:* 6 mg
Fat: 9.7 g   *Sodium:* 815 mg

CREAMY SPINACH PESTO

This surprising alternative to the traditional all-basil pesto gains its deep green color from fresh spinach and extra richness from reduced chicken broth and low-fat hoop cheese.

Serve over thin-to-medium strands or ribbons, such as angel hair, spaghetti, linguine, or fettuccine.

4 cups packed raw spinach leaves (from ¾-pound bunch), stemmed and thoroughly washed
3 medium garlic cloves, peeled
½ pound hoop cheese
1 ounce grated Parmesan cheese
1 cup reduced chicken broth (see page 6)
2 tablespoons finely shredded fresh basil leaves
2 tablespoons finely chopped fresh Italian parsley
1 teaspoon dried oregano
¼ teaspoon freshly ground black pepper

Bring a large pot of water to a full rolling boil. Add the spinach leaves and parboil for about 30 seconds. Drain well, rinse briefly in cold running water to cool the spinach, and squeeze out as much moisture as you can from the spinach with your hands.

Put the garlic in a food processor fitted with the metal blade. Pulse the machine, stopping to scrape down the bowl, until the garlic is finely chopped. Add the spinach and all the remaining ingredients. Pulse the machine a few times to chop the spinach coarsely. Scrape down the bowl. Then process until the mixture is finely pureed.

Toss with cooked pasta the moment the pasta has been drained.

Serves 4.

Dietary information per serving (sauce only):
Calories: 98   *Cholesterol:* 6 mg
Fat: 3 g   *Sodium:* 473 mg

RED BELL PEPPER AND SUN-DRIED TOMATO PESTO

Vividly colored and flavored, this sauce makes a quick and simple lunch dish for a weekend summer afternoon.
Serve over thin-to-medium strands or ribbons.

        3 **medium red bell peppers (about 6 ounces each), roasted, peeled, stemmed, and seeded (see page 10)**
       12 **sun-dried tomatoes**
        1 **medium garlic clove, chopped fine**
        6 **tablespoons reduced chicken broth (see page 6)**
        3 **tablespoons toasted pine nuts (see page 10)**
     1½ **tablespoons finely shredded fresh basil leaves**
     1½ **tablespoons chopped fresh Italian parsley**
     1½ **tablespoons lemon juice**
        ½ **tablespoon sugar**
        1 **ounce grated Parmesan cheese**

Put all the ingredients in a food processor fitted with the metal blade. Turning the machine on and off rapidly, pulse the ingredients several times until coarsely chopped. Scrape down the work bowl. Then process continuously until the sauce is smooth. If the pesto seems too thick, pulse in a little hot water.

Toss with cooked pasta the moment the pasta has been drained.

Serves 4

Dietary information per serving (sauce only):
Calories: 138   *Cholesterol:* 5 mg
Fat: 6.5 g   *Sodium:* 241 mg

LIGHT BASIL PESTO

The classic Genovese sauce is lightened here by reducing some of its more caloric, higher-fat ingredients—the olive oil, Parmesan, and pine nuts—and adding some reduced chicken broth to enrich the flavor. Several of my testers swore they preferred this version to more conventional pestos.

Serve the sauce over delicate-to-medium strands or ribbons of pasta, such as angel hair, spaghetti, linguine, or fettuccine.

- 3 **cups packed stemmed fresh basil leaves**
- ½ **cup grated Parmesan cheese**
- 6 **tablespoons toasted pine nuts (see page 10)**
- 6 **tablespoons olive oil**
- ½ **cup reduced chicken broth (see page 6)**
- 3 **medium garlic cloves**

Put all the ingredients into a food processor fitted with the metal blade. Turning the machine on and off rapidly, pulse the ingredients several times until coarsely chopped. Scrape down the work bowl. Then process continuously until the sauce is smooth. If the pesto seems too thick, pulse in a little hot water.

Toss with cooked pasta the moment the pasta has been drained.

Serves 4

Dietary information per serving (sauce only):
Calories: 353   *Cholesterol:* 10 mg
Fat: 32 g   *Sodium:* 338 mg

2
SEAFOOD SAUCES

TUNA NIÇOISE

SALSA TONNATO

TUNA AND FAVA BEANS

TUNA, PEAS, AND FRESH TOMATO

TUNA AND MUSHROOM CREAM

SWORDFISH WITH FENNEL AND TOMATOES

GRILLED SALMON WITH TOMATO-DILL MARINARA

SMOKED SALMON WITH YOGURT AND LEMON

CAJUN SHRIMP JAMBALAYA

LIGHT SHRIMP SCAMPI

BAY SCALLOP SAUTE

SCALLOPS WITH SPINACH AND TOMATOES

SPICY CRAB

RED CLAM

WHITE CLAM

MUSSELS WITH SAFFRON AND TOMATOES

CAVIAR WITH SHALLOTS AND OLIVE OIL

TUNA NIÇOISE

Here's a quick, simple, Mediterranean-style sauce based on canned tuna. Of course, part of its lightness depends on selecting a good brand of water-packed, rather than oil-packed, tuna, and on using low-salt, water-packed black olives.
Serve over medium-sized strands, ribbons, tubes, or shapes.

1 tablespoon olive oil
2 medium shallots, chopped fine
1 medium garlic clove, chopped fine
1 small (3-ounce) onion, coarsely chopped
1 small (5-ounce) green bell pepper, halved,
    stemmed, seeded, and cut into ½-inch chunks
1 16-ounce can salt-free whole tomatoes
2 tablespoons balsamic or red-wine vinegar
1 tablespoon double-concentrate tomato paste
2 teaspoons sugar
½ tablespoon dried oregano
½ tablespoon dried basil
1 6½-ounce can white tuna in spring water, broken
    into rough (½- to ¾-inch) chunks
1 cup (about 48) medium-sized canned, low-salt,
    pitted black olives, drained and broken into halves
    by hand
2 tablespoons capers, drained and rinsed
2 tablespoons finely chopped fresh Italian parsley
Freshly ground black pepper

    In a large skillet or saucepan, heat the oil over moderate heat. Add the shallots, garlic, onion, and bell pepper and sauté until they begin to brown, 5 to 7 minutes.
    Add the tomatoes, crushing them with your hands, and stir in the vinegar, tomato paste, sugar, oregano, and basil. Simmer until thick but still slightly

liquid, about 7 minutes. Then gently stir in the tuna, olives, capers, and parsley and simmer until thick and thoroughly heated through, 5 to 7 minutes more.

Spoon over cooked pasta and season to taste with plenty of black pepper.

Serves 4

Dietary information per serving (sauce only):
Calories: 206   *Cholesterol:* 0 mg
Fat: 8 g   *Sodium:* 668 mg

SALSA TONNATO

This smooth, creamy puree of water-packed tuna and light mayonnaise, seasoned with capers, lemon juice, and herbs, recalls the classic Italian tonnato *sauce often used to dress appetizers of cold roasted veal. A room-temperature sauce, it should be tossed with the pasta the instant it is drained.*

Serve with thin-to-medium strands or ribbons.

2 6½-ounce cans white tuna in spring water
½ cup light mayonnaise
2 tablespoons capers, drained and rinsed
2 tablespoons lemon juice
2 tablespoons coarsely chopped fresh Italian parsley
2 tablespoons coarsely chopped fresh chives
Freshly ground black pepper

Put all the ingredients in a food processor fitted with the metal blade. Pulse the machine several times. Scrape down the sides of the bowl, then continue processing until smooth.

Toss the sauce with cooked pasta as soon as the pasta is drained.

Serves 4

Dietary information per serving (sauce only):
Calories: 220   *Cholesterol:* 0 mg
Fat: 11.7 g   *Sodium:* 733 mg

TUNA AND FAVA BEANS

Credit for this terrific sauce goes to my wife, Katie. When I created a Tuna and White Beans sauce for my book Pasta Presto, *she immediately came up with her own variation using fresh fava beans, which she loves. We've been eating the dish that way ever since, and I found it took well to further lightening by substituting water-packed tuna for oil-packed, and by replacing some of the olive oil with a little fish stock. Katie approves.*

Incidentally, once the fava beans are removed from their pods, we never peel off the thick skins from the individual beans. We enjoy their slightly chewy texture.

Serve over spaghetti, linguine, tagliatelli, fettuccine, or with medium shells, bow ties, or other shapes.

- 1¼ **pounds fresh fava beans in their pods, shelled (about 6½ ounces shelled beans)**
- 2 **tablespoons olive oil**
- 2 **medium garlic cloves, chopped fine**
- 6 **tablespoons rich, salt-free fish stock**
- ¼ **cup lemon juice**
- 1 **6½-ounce can white tuna in spring water, broken into rough (½- to ¾-inch) chunks**
- ¼ **cup finely chopped fresh Italian parsley**
- **Freshly ground black pepper**

Bring a medium saucepan of water to a boil. Add the shelled fava beans and parboil them until tender-crisp, about 3 minutes. Drain well.

In a large skillet, heat the oil with the garlic over moderate heat. When the garlic sizzles, add the fava beans, fish stock, and lemon juice.

As soon as the liquid simmers, pour it and the beans over cooked pasta. Scatter the tuna on top and garnish with parsley and plenty of black pepper.

Serves 4

Dietary information per serving (sauce only):
Calories: 163   *Cholesterol:* 0 mg
Fat: 7.8 g   *Sodium:* 287 mg

TUNA, PEAS, AND FRESH TOMATO

Fresh and light-tasting, this is a great sauce to make when tomatoes are at their most flavorful.

Serve over spaghetti, linguine, tagliatelli, fettuccine, or with medium shells, bow ties, or other shapes.

> 1 tablespoon olive oil
> 2 medium garlic cloves, chopped fine
> 1 cup rich, salt-free fish stock
> 6 ounces peas in the pod, shelled (about ½ cup peas)
> 1 6½-ounce can white tuna in spring water, broken into rough (½- to ¾-inch) chunks
> 1 medium-to-large firm ripe tomato, peeled, cored, seeded (see page 9), and cut into ¼-inch dice
> 1½ tablespoons finely chopped fresh Italian parsley
> 2 teaspoons finely chopped fresh savory leaves
> 2 teaspoons lemon juice
> Freshly ground black pepper

In a medium saucepan, heat the oil with the garlic over moderate heat. When the garlic sizzles, add the stock. As soon as the stock simmers briskly, add the peas, reduce the heat slightly, cover, and cook until they are tender, 3 to 4 minutes.

Add the tuna, tomato, herbs, and lemon juice to the pan. Simmer for 30 seconds to 1 minute more, then pour over cooked pasta. Season generously with black pepper.

Serves 4

Dietary information per serving (sauce only):
Calories: 120   *Cholesterol:* 0 mg
Fat: 4.4 g   *Sodium:* 298 mg

TUNA AND MUSHROOM CREAM

If truth be told, this was conceived as a light version of the tuna-noodle casserole we all ate in our childhoods. The only difference is, the heavy-duty creamed soup has been replaced by evaporated nonfat milk.

Serve over medium-to-wide ribbons, or over medium-to-large tubes, shells, or other shapes.

> **2 tablespoons corn oil**
> **4 medium shallots, chopped fine**
> **2 medium garlic cloves, chopped fine**
> **½ pound button mushrooms, cut into ¼-inch slices**
> **1 cup evaporated nonfat milk**
> **1 ounce grated Parmesan cheese**
> **1 6½-ounce can white tuna in spring water, broken into rough (½- to ¾-inch) chunks**
> **2 tablespoons finely chopped fresh Italian parsley**
> **1 tablespoon finely chopped fresh chives**
> **Freshly ground black pepper**

In a large saucepan or skillet, heat the oil with the shallots and garlic over moderate heat. When the vegetables sizzle, raise the heat to high and add the mushrooms, sautéing just until they begin to brown, 4 to 5 minutes.

Reduce the heat and add the evaporated milk. Simmer briskly, stirring frequently to guard against boiling over, until the milk reduces by about a third, to a creamy consistency, 5 to 7 minutes.

Stir in the Parmesan cheese and, as soon as it melts, fold in the tuna and herbs. Simmer just until the tuna is heated through, then spoon over cooked pasta. Season with black pepper to taste.

Serves 4

Dietary information per serving (sauce only):
Calories: 222   *Cholesterol:* 8 mg
Fat: 9.8 g   *Sodium:* 422 mg

SWORDFISH WITH FENNEL AND TOMATOES

The sweet, meaty flavor of swordfish is complemented here by strips of fresh bulb fennel in a tomato sauce enhanced by fish stock.
Serve over medium strands, ribbons, or shapes.

2 tablespoons olive oil
2 medium shallots, chopped fine
2 medium garlic cloves, chopped fine
6 ounces bulb fennel, cut into ¼-by-½-inch pieces
1 16-ounce can salt-free whole tomatoes
½ cup rich, salt-free fish stock
1 tablespoon double-concentrate tomato paste
1½ tablespoons chopped fresh Italian parsley
1 tablespoon sugar
2 teaspoons dried marjoram
2 teaspoons lemon juice
1 teaspoon whole fennel seeds
1 bay leaf
½ pound fresh swordfish fillet, cut into ½-inch pieces

In a large saucepan or skillet, heat the olive oil over moderate heat. Add the shallots, garlic, and fennel and sauté about 2 minutes. Add the tomatoes, crushing them with your hands, and stir in the fish stock, tomato paste, parsley, sugar, marjoram, lemon juice, fennel seeds, and bay leaf.

As soon as the sauce begins to simmer, stir in the chunks of swordfish. Continue simmering until the sauce is thick but still fairly liquid, 10 to 15 minutes. Spoon over cooked pasta.

Serves 4

Dietary information per serving (sauce only):
Calories: 205   *Cholesterol:* 22 mg
Fat: 9.4 g   *Sodium:* 121 mg

GRILLED SALMON WITH TOMATO-DILL MARINARA

Plan to serve this vibrant, elegant topping as a special main course at dinner. Buy the best, freshest salmon fillets you can find and have them cut into ½-inch-thick medallions that will grill quickly.

Serve over fine strands—angel hair or spaghettini.

- 3 tablespoons olive oil
- 2 tablespoons lemon juice
- 1 pound fresh salmon fillets, cut into ½-inch-thick medallions
- 2 medium shallots, chopped fine
- 1 medium garlic clove, chopped fine
- 1 16-ounce can salt-free whole tomatoes
- ½ cup rich, salt-free fish stock
- 1 tablespoon double-concentrate tomato paste
- 1 tablespoon finely chopped fresh dillweed
- 1 tablespoon finely chopped fresh Italian parsley
- 2 teaspoons sugar
- 1 bay leaf
- 1 tablespoon chopped fresh chives

In a mixing bowl, stir together 2 tablespoons of the olive oil with the lemon juice. Turn the salmon fillets in the mixture to coat them, and leave them to marinate for about 30 minutes, turning them two or three times.

Preheat the broiler.

While the salmon marinates and the broiler heats, prepare the sauce. In a large saucepan or skillet, heat the remaining olive oil with the shallots and garlic over moderate heat. When the vegetables begin to sizzle, add the tomatoes, crushing them with your hands, and stir in the fish stock, tomato paste, dill, parsley, sugar, and bay leaf. Simmer until thick but still slightly liquid, about 20 minutes.

While the sauce is still simmering, remove the salmon from the marinade, discarding the marinade. Broil the salmon close to the heat until golden brown, about 3 minutes per side.

Spoon the sauce over individual servings of cooked pasta. Place the salmon medallions on top of the sauce and garnish with chives.

Serves 4

Dietary information per serving (sauce only):
Calories: 275   *Cholesterol:* 62 mg
Fat: 14 g   *Sodium:* 121 mg

SMOKED SALMON WITH YOGURT AND LEMON

Serve this elegant cousin to a pasta salad for brunch or lunch, tossed with medium strands, such as linguine or spaghetti. Use lemon juice if you want a milder lemon flavor, zest if you prefer it stronger.

> **2 cups plain low-fat yogurt, at room temperature**
> **¼ pound thinly sliced smoked salmon, cut crosswise into ¼-inch-wide strips**
> **4 teaspoons lemon juice or zest**
> **1½ tablespoons finely chopped fresh chives**
> **Freshly ground black pepper**

Toss cooked pasta with the yogurt. Scatter the salmon strips on top, then sprinkle with lemon juice or zest and scatter with chives. Season to taste with black pepper.

Serves 4

Dietary information per serving (sauce only):
Calories: 105   *Cholesterol:* 13 mg
Fat: 3.3 g   *Sodium:* 308 mg

CAJUN SHRIMP JAMBALAYA

A sauce inspired by a favorite New Orleans dish.
 Serve over medium ribbons such as fettuccine, or over medium shapes such as bow ties or shells.

- 2 tablespoons olive oil
- 4 medium garlic cloves, chopped fine
- 1 small (3-ounce) onion, coarsely chopped
- 1 small (5-ounce) green bell pepper, halved, stemmed, seeded, and cut into ½-inch chunks
- 1 pound medium-sized shrimp in the shell, shelled and deveined (about ¾ pound shrimp meat)
- 1 16-ounce can salt-free whole tomatoes
- 1 tablespoon double-concentrate tomato paste
- 2 teaspoons sugar
- 2 teaspoons dried oregano
- ½ teaspoon ground red pepper
- ¾ teaspoon ground cumin
- ½ teaspoon ground white pepper
- 1 bay leaf
- ¼ pound fresh okra, trimmed and cut into ½-inch pieces
- ¼ cup finely chopped fresh Italian parsley

In a large skillet or saucepan, heat the olive oil over moderate heat. Add the garlic, onion, and bell pepper and sauté until they begin to brown, 5 to 7 minutes. Add the shrimp and sauté just until they begin to turn pink, 1 to 2 minutes more.

Add the tomatoes, crushing them with your hands, and stir in the tomato paste, sugar, oregano, red pepper, cumin, white pepper, and bay leaf. When the liquid starts to simmer, stir in the okra and continue simmering until the sauce is thick but still slightly liquid, 7 to 10 minutes.

Stir in the parsley and spoon over cooked pasta.

Serves 4

Dietary information per serving (sauce only):
Calories: 223   *Cholesterol:* 129 mg
Fat: 8.8 g   *Sodium:* 189 mg

LIGHT SHRIMP SCAMPI

The traditional scampi-style pasta topping calls for quite a bit of oil. This version cuts the oil down to a minimum and lightens the sauce with white wine and rich fish stock.

Serve over fine-to-medium strands.

- **2 tablespoons olive oil**
- **4 medium garlic cloves, chopped fine**
- **1 pound medium-sized shrimp in the shell, shelled and deveined (about ¾ pound shrimp meat)**
- **1 cup rich, salt-free fish stock**
- **½ cup dry white wine**
- **¼ cup finely chopped fresh Italian parsley**
- **4 teaspoons finely grated fresh lemon zest**
- **2 teaspoons cornstarch**
- **¼ cup lemon juice**
- **Freshly ground black pepper**

In a large skillet, heat the oil with the garlic over moderate-to-high heat. When the garlic sizzles, add the shrimp and sauté just until they turn pink, about 1 minute. Stir in the fish stock, wine, parsley, and lemon zest.

In a small cup or bowl, stir the cornstarch into the lemon juice until it dissolves, then stir that mixture into the ingredients in the skillet. Simmer until the sauce begins to thicken slightly, about 1 minute.

Spoon the sauce over cooked pasta. Season generously with black pepper.

Serves 4

Dietary information per serving (sauce only):
Calories: 191   *Cholesterol:* 129 mg
Fat: 8.3 g   *Sodium:* 160 mg

BAY SCALLOP SAUTE

Sweet and succulent, little bay scallops taste rich and sinful, yet they're low in calories and relatively low in cholesterol and sodium. They feature here in a quick sauté with a colorful confetti of bell peppers, garnished with a sprinkling of pine nuts and fresh basil. (If you have trouble locating different-colored bell peppers, by all means use just one color.)

Serve over fine-to-medium strands or ribbons, such as angel hair, spaghetti, linguine, or fettuccine.

1 tablespoon olive oil
1 medium garlic clove, chopped fine
¾ pound bay scallops
¼ medium red bell pepper, cut into ¼-inch dice
¼ medium green bell pepper, cut into ¼-inch dice
¼ medium yellow bell pepper, cut into ¼-inch dice
½ cup rich, salt-free fish stock
¼ cup dry white wine
2 teaspoons cornstarch
¼ cup finely shredded fresh basil leaves
2 tablespoons toasted pine nuts (see page 10)
Freshly ground black pepper

In a large skillet, heat the oil with the garlic over moderate-to-high heat. When the garlic sizzles, add the scallops and sauté just until they firm up slightly, about 30 seconds. Then add the peppers and sauté about 1 minute more.

Stir in the fish stock. In a small cup or bowl, stir the cornstarch into the wine until it dissolves, then stir that mixture into the ingredients in the skillet. Simmer until the sauce begins to thicken slightly, about 1 minute. Then stir in the basil and pine nuts and spoon over cooked pasta. Season to taste with black pepper.

Serves 4

Dietary information per serving (sauce only):
Calories: 158   *Cholesterol:* 28 mg
Fat: 6.8 g   *Sodium:* 155 mg

SCALLOPS WITH SPINACH AND TOMATOES

This vividly flavored yet casual sauce is excellent served over medium strands or ribbons, such as spaghetti, linguine, or fettuccine.

- 1 tablespoon olive oil
- 2 medium garlic cloves, chopped fine
- 1 16-ounce can salt-free whole tomatoes
- ½ cup rich, salt-free fish stock
- 1 tablespoon lemon juice
- 1 tablespoon double-concentrate tomato paste
- 2 teaspoons sugar
- 1 bay leaf
- ½ pound bay scallops
- ¼ pound spinach leaves (about 1 cup packed), stemmed, ribbed, thoroughly washed, and cut crosswise into ½-inch-wide strips

In a large skillet or saucepan, heat the oil with the garlic over moderate heat. When the garlic sizzles, add the tomatoes, crushing them with your hands, and stir in the fish stock, lemon juice, tomato paste, sugar, and bay leaf.

Simmer for 7 to 10 minutes, until thick but still fairly liquid. Then stir in the scallops and the spinach and continue simmering until the scallops are cooked through and the sauce is thick, 3 to 5 minutes more. Serve over cooked pasta.

Serves 4

Dietary information per serving (sauce only):
Calories: 132   *Cholesterol:* 19 mg
Fat: 3.9 g   *Sodium:* 182 mg

SPICY CRAB

There's something about the sweet, rich flavor of crab that just calls for a good dose of spice. If you prefer things less spicy, feel free to skimp on the red pepper flakes. Be sure to add the crabmeat near the end of the cooking process, to preserve its texture.

Serve over medium strands or ribbons, such as spaghetti, linguine, fettuccine, or fettuccelli.

>   1 tablespoon olive oil
>   2 medium garlic cloves, chopped fine
>   ½ medium green bell pepper, cut into ¼-inch dice
>   1 teaspoon crushed red pepper flakes
>   1 16-ounce can salt-free whole tomatoes
>   ½ cup rich, salt-free fish stock
>   1 tablespoon double-concentrate tomato paste
>   1 tablespoon finely chopped fresh parsley
>   2 teaspoons sugar
>   1 teaspoon finely grated lemon zest
>   1 bay leaf
>   ½ pound flaked crabmeat

In a large skillet or saucepan, heat the oil with the garlic, bell pepper, and red pepper flakes over moderate heat. When they sizzle, add the tomatoes, crushing them with your hands, and stir in the fish stock, tomato paste, parsley, sugar, lemon zest, and bay leaf.

Simmer for 7 to 10 minutes, until thick but still fairly liquid. Then stir in the crabmeat and continue simmering until the sauce is thick, 3 to 5 minutes more. Serve over cooked pasta.

Serves 4

Dietary information per serving (sauce only):
Calories: 138   *Cholesterol:* 30 mg
Fat: 6.7 g   *Sodium:* 686 mg

RED CLAM

One of the classic pasta sauces is lightened here by reducing the amount of oil and adding fish stock and a splash of red wine. Be sure to serve this sauce in shallow soup bowls, to catch all the delicious wine-and-tomato-flavored broth.
Serve in the classic style, over linguine or spaghetti.

2 tablespoons olive oil
4 medium garlic cloves, chopped fine
1 cup rich, salt-free fish stock
1 cup dry red wine
2 teaspoons dried oregano
3 dozen small fresh clams, such as littlenecks or Manilas, in the shell, thoroughly cleaned
1 large (8- to 9-ounce) firm ripe tomato, peeled, cored, seeded (see page 9), and coarsely chopped
2 tablespoons double-concentrate tomato paste
1½ tablespoons finely shredded fresh basil leaves
1½ tablespoons finely chopped fresh Italian parsley
Freshly ground black pepper

In a large saucepan, heat the oil with the garlic over moderate heat. When the garlic sizzles, add the fish stock, wine, and oregano.

As soon as the liquid comes to a boil, add the clams and cover the pan. Steam the clams until all of them have opened, 3 to 5 minutes; discard any unopened clams. With a slotted spoon, remove them from the pan and keep them warm in a covered bowl.

Stir the remaining ingredients, except the black pepper, into the liquid in the pan. As soon as the liquid returns to a simmer, place the clams, shells and all, on top of cooked pasta and spoon the liquid over them. Season to taste with black pepper.

Serves 4

Dietary information per serving (sauce only):
Calories: 196   *Cholesterol:* 20 mg
Fat: 7.6 g   *Sodium:* 148 mg

WHITE CLAM

In this alternative to the classic clam sauce, the shellfish are presented in a rich yet light broth of fish stock and white wine. Be sure to serve this sauce in shallow soup bowls, to catch all the delicious wine-flavored broth.

Serve over linguine or spaghetti.

- **2 tablespoons olive oil**
- **3 medium garlic cloves, chopped fine**
- **1 cup rich, salt-free fish stock**
- **1 cup dry white wine**
- **3 dozen small fresh clams, such as littlenecks or Manilas, in the shell, thoroughly cleaned**
- **¼ cup finely chopped fresh Italian parsley**
- **Freshly ground black pepper**

In a large saucepan, heat the oil with the garlic over moderate heat. When the garlic sizzles, add the fish stock and wine.

As soon as the liquid comes to a boil, add the clams and cover the pan. Steam the clams until all of them have opened, 3 to 5 minutes; discard any unopened clams. With a slotted spoon, remove them from the pan and place them, shells and all, on top of cooked pasta.

Stir the parsley into the liquid in the pan and spoon the liquid over the clams and pasta. Season to taste with black pepper.

Serves 4

Dietary information per serving (sauce only):
Calories: 155   *Cholesterol:* 20 mg
Fat: 7.3 g   *Sodium:* 68 mg

MUSSELS WITH SAFFRON AND TOMATOES

The exotic perfume of imported saffron is a natural with the sweet flavor of mussels. In this light recipe, the two are joined in a tomato sauce enriched with fish stock. Serve over spaghetti or linguine.

2 tablespoons olive oil
3 medium garlic cloves, chopped fine
½ cup rich, salt-free fish stock
1 generous pinch saffron threads
32 small (about 2-inch-long) fresh mussels in the shell, rinsed clean and debearded
1 16-ounce can salt-free whole tomatoes
1 tablespoon double-concentrate tomato paste
1 tablespoon sugar
1 bay leaf
2 tablespoons finely chopped fresh chives

In a large saucepan, heat the olive oil with the garlic over moderate heat. Add the stock and the saffron and bring to a boil. Add the mussels, cover the pan, and steam until all the mussels have opened, 2 to 3 minutes; discard any unopened mussels. With a slotted spoon, remove the mussels from the pan and keep them warm in a covered bowl.

Add the tomatoes to the pan, breaking them up with your hands, and stir in the remaining ingredients, except for the chives. Simmer briskly until the sauce is thick but fairly liquid, 5 to 7 minutes. Then return the mussels to the pan and simmer to warm them through, about 1 minute more.

Spoon the sauce, shells and all, over cooked pasta. Garnish with chives.

Serves 4

Dietary information per serving (sauce only):
Calories: 162   *Cholesterol:* 16 mg
Fat: 8.1 g   *Sodium:* 180 mg

CAVIAR WITH SHALLOTS AND OLIVE OIL

It's the epitome of elegance, yet it needn't be extravagantly expensive: You can use American golden caviar or salmon caviar in this recipe, instead of costly imported varieties. Serve this topping for a candlelit supper, or at a luncheon table set with your finest china and silver.

Serve over angel hair or spaghettini.

¼ **cup olive oil**
4 **medium shallots, chopped fine**
¼ **cup American golden caviar**
1½ **tablespoons finely chopped fresh chives**

In a medium skillet, heat the oil with the shallots over moderate heat. As soon as the shallots sizzle, pour them with the oil over individual servings of pasta. Top each serving with a dollop of caviar and a sprinkling of chives.

Serves 4

Dietary information per serving (sauce only):
Calories: 165   *Cholesterol:* 83 mg
Fat: 16 g   *Sodium:* 212 mg

3

POULTRY AND MEAT SAUCES

CHICKEN AND RED BELL PEPPER BOLOGNESE

GRILLED CHICKEN WITH FRESH OREGANO PESTO
AND TOMATO

CHICKEN CACCIATORE

CHICKEN BABA GHANOOSH

CHICKEN TIKKA WITH MINT RAITA

FAJITA-STYLE CHICKEN WITH TOMATILLO-TOMATO SALSA

CHINESE-STYLE CHICKEN SAUTE

CHOPPED CHICKEN AND PEAS IN BROTH

MEXICAN CHICKEN MEATBALLS WITH
TOMATOES AND JALAPEÑOS

TURKEY BOLOGNESE

TURKEY A LA KING

ITALIAN-STYLE TURKEY SAUSAGE WITH GREEN PEPPERS

STIR-FRIED DUCK WITH GINGER AND SHIITAKE
MUSHROOMS

LIGHT BEEF BOLOGNESE

EXTRALEAN BEEF MEATBALLS NAPOLITANO

BEEFSTEAK STROGANOFF

GRILLED BEEF FILLET WITH ROASTED PEPPER PESTO

GROUND VEAL WITH MUSHROOMS IN TOMATO CREAM

VEAL-AND-ROSEMARY MEATBALLS WITH
CHERRY TOMATOES

LAMB AND EGGPLANT WITH SPICED YOGURT

LAMB OREGANATO

HAM AND BLACK-EYED PEAS IN BROTH

DICED HAM WITH BITTER GREENS,
SHALLOTS, AND TOMATOES

SWEET-AND-SOUR GROUND PORK

CHICKEN AND RED BELL PEPPER BOLOGNESE

The classic Bolognese sauce is based on tomatoes and ground meat—usually beef (see Light Beef Bolognese on page 98). This lighter version replaces the beef with ground chicken breast and complements the chicken's flavor with the addition of roasted red bell peppers. Many supermarkets sell ready-ground chicken breast meat these days; but, for the lowest calorie count, be sure to check with your butcher that all the fat and skin were trimmed away before the meat was ground. If you can't be sure, or if ground chicken isn't available in your market, simply buy boneless, skinless chicken breasts—or bone and skin them yourself—and then trim off all visible fat and chop the meat in a food processor fitted with the metal blade.

Serve over medium strands or ribbons, such as spaghetti or fettuccine, or over medium-sized tubes, shells, or other shapes.

1 tablespoon olive oil
1 small onion (about 3 ounces), chopped fine
1 medium garlic clove, chopped fine
½ pound ground chicken breast
½ cup Chardonnay or other dry white wine
1 16-ounce can salt-free whole tomatoes
1 tablespoon double-concentrate tomato paste
1 tablespoon finely shredded fresh basil leaves
1 tablespoon finely chopped fresh Italian parsley
2 teaspoons sugar
1 teaspoon finely chopped fresh rosemary leaves
2 medium red bell peppers (about 6 ounces each),
  roasted, peeled, stemmed, seeded (see page 10),
  and coarsely chopped, juices saved

In a large saucepan or skillet, heat the olive oil with the onion and garlic over moderate heat. When they sizzle, add the chicken and sauté it, stirring and breaking up the meat with a wooden spoon, until it begins to brown, 5 to 7 minutes.

Add the wine and stir and scrape well to deglaze the pan. Add the tomatoes, breaking them up with your hands, and stir in the remaining ingredients.

Simmer the sauce until thick but still slightly liquid, 20 to 25 minutes. Spoon over cooked pasta.

Serves 4

Dietary information per serving (sauce only):
Calories: 164   *Cholesterol:* 30 mg
Fat: 3.7 g   *Sodium:* 107 mg

GRILLED CHICKEN WITH FRESH OREGANO PESTO AND TOMATO

Simple, fresh-tasting, and elegant, this topping exemplifies the way in which contemporary cooking can be both light and wonderfully flavorful. Fresh oregano is available in most well-stocked produce sections these days, but if you can't find any, you can substitute half the quantity of dried oregano.

Serve over fine-to-medium strands or ribbons, such as angel hair, spaghettini, linguine, spaghetti, tagliatelli, or fettuccine.

¼ cup plus 1 tablespoon olive oil
1 tablespoon lemon juice
1 pound boneless, skinless chicken breasts, trimmed of all visible fat
1 cup packed stemmed fresh basil leaves
½ cup packed fresh Italian parsley leaves
¼ cup packed fresh oregano leaves
¼ cup toasted pine nuts (see page 10)
¼ cup reduced chicken broth (see page 6)
1 ounce grated Parmesan cheese
2 medium garlic cloves
1 large tomato (8 to 9 ounces), stemmed and coarsely chopped

In a mixing bowl, stir 1 tablespoon of the oil with the lemon juice. Add the chicken breasts and turn them in the mixture; leave them to marinate for about half an hour.

Remove the broiler tray and spray it lightly with nonstick cooking spray. Preheat the broiler without the tray.

Put the chicken on the tray and broil it until golden, about 7 minutes per side.

While the chicken is broiling, make the pesto. Put the remaining oil, basil, parsley, oregano, pine nuts, broth, Parmesan, and garlic in a food processor fitted with the metal blade. Pulse the ingredients several times until coarsely chopped. Scrape down the work bowl. Then process continuously until the sauce is smooth. If the pesto seems too thick, pulse in a little hot water.

Spoon the pesto over cooked pasta. Cut the chicken crosswise into ¼-inch-wide strips and place them on top of the pesto. Garnish with chopped tomato.

Serves 4

Dietary information per serving (sauce only):
Calories: 361   *Cholesterol:* 65 mg
Fat: 29 g   *Sodium:* 194 mg

CHICKEN CACCIATORE

Cooked "huntsman-style," this sauce is inspired by the popular Italian stew.
Serve over medium strands, ribbons, tubes, or shapes.

- 1½ tablespoons olive oil
- 2 medium garlic cloves, chopped fine
- ½ small green bell pepper, cut into ½-by-1-inch strips
- ½ small onion, cut into ½-inch dice
- 2 ounces small button mushrooms, left whole or halved, depending on size
- ½ pound boneless, skinless chicken breasts, trimmed of all fat and cut crosswise into ½-inch-wide strips
- ¼ cup dry red wine
- ¼ cup reduced chicken broth (see page 6)
- 1 16-ounce can salt-free whole tomatoes
- 1 tablespoon double-concentrate tomato paste
- 1 tablespoon finely chopped fresh Italian parsley
- ½ tablespoon sugar
- 1 teaspoon dried basil
- 1 teaspoon dried oregano
- 1 bay leaf

In a large skillet or saucepan, heat 1 tablespoon of the oil over high heat. Add the garlic, pepper, onion, and mushrooms; sauté until they are tender and just beginning to brown, about 3 minutes.

Remove the vegetables and set them aside. Add the remaining oil and, still over high heat, sauté the chicken strips until they begin to turn golden, about 2 minutes.

Add the wine and broth, and stir and scrape to deglaze the skillet. Add the tomatoes, breaking them up with your hands, and stir in the remaining ingredients.

Simmer the sauce until it is thick but still slightly liquid, about 20 minutes. Serve over cooked pasta.

Serves 4

Dietary information per serving (sauce only):
Calories: 162   *Cholesterol:* 30 mg
Fat: 7.6 g   *Sodium:* 194 mg

CHICKEN BABA GHANOOSH

Baba ghanoosh is a classic Middle Eastern spread of pureed roasted eggplant with a voluptuous texture that belies how light it really is. It seemed to me to go marvelously with a topping of marinated, grilled chicken.
Serve over medium-to-large ribbons or shapes.

> **3 tablespoons lemon juice**
> **1 tablespoon olive oil**
> **1 teaspoon dried oregano**
> **4 medium garlic cloves, 1 chopped fine, 3 left whole**
> **1 pound boneless, skinless chicken breasts, trimmed
>   of all visible fat**
> **1 large eggplant (about 1½ pounds)**
> **⅓ cup packed fresh Italian parsley leaves**
> **⅓ cup low-fat yogurt**
> **Freshly ground black pepper**

In a mixing bowl, stir 1 tablespoon of the lemon juice with the oil, oregano, and the chopped garlic clove. Add the chicken breasts and turn them in the mixture; leave them to marinate for about half an hour.

Meanwhile, roast the eggplant by spearing it on a large fork and slowly, carefully turning it over an open flame on your stovetop until its skin is evenly blistered and blackened, about 15 minutes. (Alternatively, you can roast it for about 15 minutes under the broiler.) Let the eggplant stand until it is cool enough to handle, then peel off the skin.

Remove the broiler tray and spray it lightly with nonstick cooking spray. (Be sure the tray is cool first, if you used it for the eggplant.) Preheat the broiler without the tray.

Put the chicken on the tray and broil it until golden, about 7 minutes per side.

While the chicken is broiling, make the baba ghanoosh. Put the remaining garlic cloves and the parsley in a food processor fitted with the metal blade and pulse the ingredients until they are coarsely chopped. Add the peeled eggplant, yogurt, and remaining lemon juice and process until the mixture is smoothly pureed.

Toss the eggplant puree with cooked pasta in a skillet over low-to-moderate heat just until warmed through. As soon as the chicken is done, cut it into rough ½-inch chunks and scatter it on top of the pasta. Season generously to taste with black pepper.

Serves 4

Dietary information per serving (sauce only):
Calories: 185   *Cholesterol:* 61 mg
Fat: 8.4 g   *Sodium:* 128 mg

CHICKEN TIKKA WITH MINT RAITA

Though chicken tikka is traditionally grilled in a specially built Indian oven, this recipe produces similarly succulent and flavorful results with a home broiler. I've adapted the Indian recipe into a pasta topping by saucing it with the yogurt-and-cucumber salad known as raita, given extra flavor here by the addition of fresh mint leaves.

Serve over medium-to-large strands or ribbons.

2 cups low-fat yogurt
4 teaspoons lemon juice
2 teaspoons grated fresh ginger root
1 teaspoon ground coriander
1 teaspoon sweet paprika
½ teaspoon ground cumin
¼ teaspoon ground turmeric
1 pound boneless, skinless chicken breasts, trimmed of all visible fat
1 small Maui onion or other sweet, mild onion, chopped fine
½ pound pickling cucumbers, unpeeled and coarsely shredded
1½ tablespoons finely chopped fresh mint leaves
1½ tablespoons finely chopped fresh cilantro leaves

In a mixing bowl, stir together ¾ cup of the yogurt and 1 teaspoon of the lemon juice with the ginger, coriander, paprika, cumin, and turmeric. Add the chicken breasts and turn them to coat them well. Leave them to marinate at room temperature for about 30 minutes, turning them once or twice.

Remove the broiler tray and spray it lightly with nonstick cooking spray. Preheat the broiler without the tray. Put the chicken on the tray and broil it until golden, about 7 minutes per side.

While the chicken is broiling, make the raita. Stir together the remaining yogurt and lemon juice with the onion, cucumber, and mint.

As soon as the chicken is done, cut it into rough 1-inch chunks. Spoon the raita over cooked pasta, top it with the chicken, and garnish with cilantro.

Serves 4

Dietary information per serving (sauce only):
Calories: 193   *Cholesterol:* 66 mg
Fat: 6.9 g   *Sodium:* 183 mg

FAJITA-STYLE CHICKEN WITH TOMATILLO-TOMATO SALSA

I've adapted the popular Southwestern dish, usually served in warm tortilla wrappers, into a light pasta topping here, sauced with a rapid sauté of fresh tomatoes and tomatillos—the green, tomatolike vegetables that are usually found encased in dry, papery, brown husks.

When handling the hot chiles, avoid touching your eyes, mouth, or any cuts lest the volatile oils cause a burning sensation, and be sure to wash your hands thoroughly with soap and water afterward.

Serve over medium strands or ribbons.

- 2 tablespoons olive oil
- ½ tablespoon lemon juice
- ½ tablespoon lime juice
- 1 teaspoon dried oregano
- 3 medium garlic cloves, chopped fine
- 2 small hot green chiles, seeded and chopped fine
- 1 pound boneless, skinless chicken breasts, trimmed of all visible fat
- 1 small red onion, coarsely chopped
- 1 small green bell pepper, coarsely chopped
- ¾ pound firm, ripe tomatoes, cored and coarsely chopped
- ½ pound firm, ripe tomatillos, husked, cored, and coarsely chopped
- 1 teaspoon sugar
- 3 tablespoons finely chopped fresh cilantro leaves

In a mixing bowl, stir 1 tablespoon of the oil with the lemon and lime juices, the oregano, 1 garlic clove, and 1 chile. Add the chicken breasts and turn them in the mixture; leave them to marinate for about half an hour.

Remove the broiler tray and spray it lightly with nonstick cooking spray. Preheat the broiler without the tray.

Put the chicken on the tray and broil it until golden, about 7 minutes per side.

While the chicken is broiling, make the salsa. In a large skillet or saucepan, heat the remaining oil with the remaining garlic and chile over moderate heat. When they sizzle, add the onion and green pepper and sauté for 2 to 3 minutes. Then add the tomatoes, tomatillos, and sugar and continue sautéing for 7 to 10 minutes until the sauce is thick but still slightly liquid.

As soon as the chicken is done, cut it crosswise into ½-inch-wide strips. Spoon the sauce over cooked pasta, top with the chicken, and sprinkle with cilantro.

Serves 4

Dietary information per serving (sauce only):
Calories: 208   *Cholesterol:* 60 mg
Fat: 11.7 g   *Sodium:* 103 mg

CHINESE-STYLE CHICKEN SAUTE

While this colorful topping is excellent over spaghetti, linguine, or fettuccine, its natural place is on top of Chinese rice or egg noodles.

2 tablespoons peanut or corn oil
1 medium garlic clove, chopped fine
½ tablespoon grated fresh ginger root
1 small carrot, cut diagonally into ⅛-inch-thick slices
½ small red bell pepper, cut into ¼-by-2-inch strips
2 ounces small snow peas, trimmed
2 ounces button mushrooms, cut into ¼-inch-thick slices
¾ pound boneless, skinless chicken breasts, trimmed of all visible fat and cut crosswise into ¼-inch-wide strips
2 tablespoons low-salt soy sauce
1 tablespoon rice-wine vinegar
1 cup reduced chicken broth (see page 6)
1 tablespoon cornstarch
2 medium scallions, sliced fine

In a large wok or skillet, heat 1 tablespoon of the oil with the garlic and ginger over high heat. As soon as they sizzle, add the carrot and stir-fry for 1 minute. Add the bell pepper and snow peas and stir-fry about 1 minute more; then add the mushrooms and stir-fry another minute.

Empty the vegetables into a mixing bowl. Heat the remaining oil in the wok, add the chicken, and stir-fry until it turns golden, about 5 minutes. Return the vegetables to the wok, add the soy sauce and vinegar, and stir and scrape with a wooden spoon to deglaze.

Add ¾ cup of the broth to the wok. Dissolve the cornstarch in the remaining broth and, as soon as the liquid in the wok simmers, stir in the cornstarch mixture. Continue simmering just until the liquid thickens to coating consistency, 1 to 2 minutes. Serve over cooked pasta, garnished with scallions.

Serves 4

Dietary information per serving (sauce only):
Calories: 185   *Cholesterol:* 45 mg
Fat: 11.1 g   *Sodium:* 729 mg

CHOPPED CHICKEN AND PEAS IN BROTH

Wonderfully homey, this simple preparation combines chunks of chicken breast with fresh peas in a rich chicken broth.
Serve it over medium-sized tubes, shells, or shapes, in shallow soup bowls.

> 1 **tablespoon olive oil**
> 1 **medium shallot, chopped fine**
> 1 **medium garlic clove, chopped fine**
> 1 **pound boneless, skinless chicken breasts, trimmed of all visible fat and cut into ½- to 1-inch chunks**
> 1½ **cups reduced chicken broth (see page 6)**
> 9 **ounces peas in the pod, shelled**
> 2 **tablespoons finely chopped fresh Italian parsley**

In a large saucepan, heat the oil with the shallot and garlic over moderate heat. When the vegetables sizzle, raise the heat to moderate-to-high and add the chicken. Continue sautéing until the chicken just begins to turn golden brown, 3 to 5 minutes.

Add the broth and the peas, reduce the heat slightly, and simmer until the peas are tender and the chicken is cooked through, about 5 minutes more. Stir in the parsley and ladle over cooked pasta.

Serves 4

Dietary information per serving (sauce only):
Calories: 171   *Cholesterol:* 60 mg
Fat: 8.8 g   *Sodium:* 618 mg

MEXICAN CHICKEN MEATBALLS WITH TOMATOES AND JALAPEÑOS

In this variation on an age-old spaghetti sauce, the meatballs are made from a spiced chicken mixture, and the tomato sauce that accompanies them has the added fire of jalapeño peppers.

For the lowest calorie count, be sure to check with your butcher that all the fat and skin was trimmed away before the chicken was ground. If you can't be sure, or if ground chicken isn't available in your market, simply buy boneless, skinless chicken breasts—or bone and skin them yourself—and then trim off all visible fat and chop the meat in a food processor fitted with the metal blade.

When handling the hot chile, avoid touching your eyes, mouth, or any cuts lest the volatile oils cause a burning sensation, and be sure to wash your hands thoroughly with soap and water afterward.

Serve over spaghetti or linguine, or with medium-sized shapes.

CHICKEN MEATBALLS

¾ **pound ground chicken breast**
2 **egg whites**
1 **tablespoon finely chopped fresh cilantro leaves**
½ **tablespoon dried oregano**
1 **teaspoon ground cumin**
1 **6-inch corn tortilla, soaked in warm water until soft, then drained**

JALAPEÑO TOMATO SAUCE

1 **tablespoon olive oil**
1 **small onion, chopped fine**
1 **medium garlic clove, chopped fine**
¾ **to 1 medium jalapeño pepper (or more to taste), stemmed, seeded, and chopped fine**

½ medium red bell pepper, cut into ¼-inch dice
1 16-ounce can salt-free whole tomatoes
2 tablespoons chopped fresh cilantro leaves
1 tablespoon double-concentrate tomato paste
2 teaspoons sugar
1 teaspoon dried oregano

Put all the ingredients for the meatballs in a mixing bowl. With your hands, squeeze the ingredients together until thoroughly blended.

Remove the broiler tray and spray it lightly with nonstick cooking spray. Preheat the broiler without the tray.

With a tablespoon and your fingers, scoop and shape rounded spoonfuls of the chicken mixture, forming balls and placing them on the broiler tray. When all the meatballs have been shaped, broil them close to the heat until golden brown, turning them over once (they'll flatten slightly)—about 5 minutes per side.

While the meatballs are broiling, start the sauce. In a large skillet or saucepan, heat the oil with the onion, garlic, jalapeño, and bell pepper over moderate heat. When the vegetables sizzle, add the tomatoes, breaking them up with your hands, and the remaining ingredients. Simmer the sauce until thick but still slightly liquid, about 10 minutes, adding the meatballs for the final few minutes of simmering.

Serve over cooked pasta.

Serves 4

Dietary information per serving (sauce only):
Calories: 190   *Cholesterol:* 45 mg
Fat: 7.3 g   *Sodium:* 156 mg

TURKEY BOLOGNESE

Ground turkey breast has so much rich flavor that you can hardly tell the difference between this sauce and the traditional beef Bolognese. Check with your butcher to make sure that the ground turkey is made from breast meat, without any fat or skin; if in doubt, buy turkey breast meat yourself and chop in a food processor.

Serve over medium strands or ribbons, such as spaghetti or fettuccine, or over medium-sized tubes, shells, or other shapes.

- **1 tablespoon olive oil**
- **1 small onion (about 3 ounces), chopped fine**
- **1 medium garlic clove, chopped fine**
- **¼ teaspoon crushed red pepper flakes**
- **½ pound ground turkey breast**
- **½ cup Chianti or other dry red wine**
- **1 16-ounce can salt-free whole tomatoes**
- **1 tablespoon double-concentrate tomato paste**
- **1 tablespoon finely shredded fresh basil leaves**
- **1 tablespoon finely chopped fresh Italian parsley**
- **2 teaspoons sugar**
- **1 teaspoon dried oregano**
- **½ teaspoon dried rosemary**
- **1 bay leaf**

In a large saucepan or skillet, heat the olive oil with the onion, garlic, and pepper flakes over moderate heat. When they sizzle, add the turkey and sauté it, stirring and breaking up the meat with a wooden spoon, until it begins to brown, 5 to 7 minutes.

Add the wine and stir and scrape well to deglaze the pan. Add the tomatoes, breaking them up with your hands, and stir in the remaining ingredients.

Simmer the sauce until thick but still slightly liquid, 20 to 25 minutes. Spoon over cooked pasta.

Serves 4

Dietary information per serving (sauce only):
Calories: 185   *Cholesterol:* 48 mg
Fat: 4 g   *Sodium:* 89 mg

TURKEY A LA KING

This favorite diner-style sauce makes a great topping for medium-sized tubes, shells, or other shapes.

    2 tablespoons corn oil
    1 small onion, chopped fine
    1 medium garlic clove, chopped fine
    ½ medium red bell pepper, cut into ¼- to ½-inch dice
    ½ medium green bell pepper, cut into ¼- to ½-inch
       dice
    ½ pound button mushrooms, cut into ¼-inch slices
    ½ pound turkey breast fillets, cut into pieces about ½
       by 1 inch
    1 cup evaporated nonfat milk
    3 tablespoons finely chopped fresh Italian parsley
    Freshly ground black pepper

In a large skillet or saucepan, heat 1 tablespoon of the oil with the onion and garlic over moderate heat. When they sizzle, raise the heat to high and add the peppers and mushrooms, sautéing just until they begin to brown, 4 to 5 minutes.

Remove the vegetables from the skillet and set them aside. Heat the remaining oil over moderate-to-high heat and add the turkey, sautéing until it just begins to turn golden brown, 3 to 5 minutes.

Reduce the heat to moderate-to-low and add the evaporated milk. Simmer briskly, stirring frequently to guard against boiling over, until the milk reduces by about a third, to a creamy consistency, 5 to 7 minutes.

Stir in the vegetables and the parsley and simmer just until the vegetables are warmed through. Then spoon over cooked pasta. Season with black pepper to taste.

Serves 4

Dietary information per serving (sauce only):
Calories: 214   *Cholesterol:* 50 mg
Fat: 7.7 g   *Sodium:* 108 mg

ITALIAN-STYLE TURKEY SAUSAGE WITH GREEN PEPPERS

Mixed with a distinctive blend of herbs and spices, ground turkey breast approximates the tangy flavor of more calorie-laden Italian pork sausage. Combined with green bell peppers in a tomato sauce, it results in a home-style dish that satisfies like all good Italian cooking. Check with your butcher to make sure that the ground turkey he or she sells is made from breast meat, without any fat or skin; if you're in any doubt, buy turkey breast meat yourself and chop in your food processor.

Serve over medium strands, ribbons, shells, or shapes.

TURKEY SAUSAGE

½ pound ground turkey breast
1 medium garlic clove, chopped fine
½ tablespoon finely chopped fresh Italian parsley
¾ teaspoon whole fennel seeds
¾ teaspoon dried oregano
⅜ teaspoon crushed red pepper flakes
½ teaspoon freshly ground black pepper
½ teaspoon sugar

SAUCE

1 tablespoon olive oil
1 small onion, chopped fine
1 medium garlic clove, chopped fine
½ medium green bell pepper, cut into ¼-by-1-inch
  strips
½ cup Chianti or other dry red wine
1 16-ounce can salt-free whole tomatoes
1 tablespoon double-concentrate tomato paste
1 teaspoon sugar
1 teaspoon dried oregano
½ teaspoon dried thyme
½ teaspoon dried marjoram

In a mixing bowl, thoroughly combine all the ingredients for the turkey sausage. Cover and refrigerate for 30 minutes to 1 hour.

To make the sauce, in a large saucepan or skillet, heat the olive oil with the onion, garlic, and green pepper over moderate heat. When the vegetables sizzle, raise the heat slightly and add the turkey sausage. Sauté it, stirring with a wooden spoon and breaking up the meat into chunks about ½ inch across, until it begins to brown, about 5 minutes.

Add the wine and stir and scrape well to deglaze the pan. Add the tomatoes, breaking them up with your hands, and stir in the remaining ingredients.

Simmer the sauce until it is thick but still slightly liquid, about 25 minutes. Spoon over cooked pasta.

Serves 4

Dietary information per serving (sauce only):
Calories: 189   *Cholesterol:* 48 mg
Fat: 4.1 g   *Sodium:* 90 mg

STIR-FRIED DUCK WITH GINGER AND SHIITAKE MUSHROOMS

Most of us think of duck as being a very fatty food indeed. But many gourmet butchers today sell duck breasts alone, and if you strip them of their skins and trim away all visible fat before cooking, you're left with a very rich-tasting and not-too-fat-laden meat that forms the basis of this elegant, Asian-influenced topping.

Serve over angel hair or spaghettini.

- **2 ounces dried shiitake mushrooms**
- **1 tablespoon peanut or corn oil**
- **2 medium scallions, sliced fine**
- **1 medium garlic clove, chopped fine**
- **2 teaspoons grated fresh ginger root**
- **¾ pound skinless, boneless duck breasts, cut crosswise into ¼-inch-thick slices**
- **2 tablespoons low-salt soy sauce**
- **1 tablespoon rice-wine vinegar**
- **1 cup reduced chicken broth (see page 6)**
- **1 tablespoon cornstarch**
- **2 tablespoons finely chopped fresh cilantro leaves**

Put the shiitakes in a small bowl and add enough warm water to cover. Leave them to soak for about 15 minutes, until soft. Then trim off and discard their stems and cut the caps into ¼-inch-wide slices.

In a wok or large skillet, heat the oil with the scallions, garlic, and ginger over high heat. As soon as they sizzle, add the duck breast and the shiitakes and stir-fry until the duck loses its pink color, about 3 minutes. Add the soy sauce and vinegar, and stir and scrape with a wooden spoon to deglaze.

Add ¾ cup of the broth to the wok. Dissolve the cornstarch in the remaining broth and, as soon as the liquid in the wok simmers, stir in the cornstarch mixture. Continue simmering just until the liquid thickens to coating consistency, 1 to 2 minutes.

Serve over cooked pasta, garnished with cilantro.

Serves 4

Dietary information per serving (sauce only):
Calories: 220   *Cholesterol:* 66 mg
Fat: 9.2 g   *Sodium:* 714 mg

LIGHT BEEF BOLOGNESE

By using the leanest ground beef available—or by chopping your own from a thoroughly trimmed lean cut of steak, like top round or eye of round—you can make a classic Bolognese sauce with rich, beefy flavor that has fewer calories than more traditional versions.

Serve over medium strands or ribbons, such as spaghetti or fettuccine, or over medium-sized tubes, shells, or other shapes.

- 1 tablespoon olive oil
- 3 medium garlic cloves, chopped fine
- 1 small onion (about 3 ounces), chopped fine
- ½ medium green bell pepper, cut into ¼-inch dice
- ½ pound leanest ground beef
- ½ cup Chianti or other dry red wine
- 1 16-ounce can salt-free whole tomatoes
- 1 tablespoon double concentrate tomato paste
- 1 tablespoon sugar
- 1 tablespoon finely chopped fresh Italian parsley
- 2 teaspoons dried oregano
- 1 teaspoon dried basil
- ½ teaspoon dried marjoram
- ¼ teaspoon dried thyme
- 1 bay leaf

In a large saucepan or skillet, heat the olive oil with the garlic, onion, and green pepper over moderate heat. When the vegetables sizzle, add the beef and sauté it, stirring and breaking up the meat with a wooden spoon, until it begins to brown, 5 to 7 minutes.

Add the wine and stir and scrape well to deglaze the pan. Add the tomatoes, breaking them up with your hands, and stir in the remaining ingredients.

Simmer the sauce until it is thick but still slightly liquid, 20 to 25 minutes. Spoon over cooked pasta.

Serves 4

Dietary information per serving (sauce only):
Calories: 224   *Cholesterol:* 35 mg
Fat: 10.5 g   *Sodium:* 90 mg

EXTRALEAN BEEF MEATBALLS NAPOLITANO

Adding some whole-wheat bread soaked in low-fat milk to the extralean meat results in moist, succulent meatballs that are a good match for the higher-calorie versions of traditional Italian cooking. If your butcher doesn't carry extralean ground beef, grind it yourself from a well-trimmed lean cut of steak, such as top round or eye of round.

Serve over spaghetti or linguine, or with medium-sized shapes.

EXTRALEAN BEEF MEATBALLS
¾ pound extralean ground beef
2 egg whites
1 slice whole-wheat bread, soaked in ¼ cup low-fat milk
1 medium shallot, chopped fine
1 tablespoon finely chopped fresh Italian parsley
½ tablespoon dried oregano
½ teaspoon freshly ground black pepper

NAPOLITANO SAUCE
1 tablespoon olive oil
1 medium shallot, chopped fine
1 medium garlic clove, chopped fine
1 16-ounce can salt-free whole tomatoes
¼ cup Chianti or other dry red wine
1 tablespoon finely shredded fresh basil leaves
1 tablespoon double-concentrate tomato paste
1 teaspoon sugar
1 teaspoon dried oregano

Put all the ingredients for the meatballs in a mixing bowl. With your hands, squeeze the ingredients together until thoroughly blended.

Remove the broiler tray and spray it lightly with nonstick cooking spray. Preheat the broiler without the tray.

With a tablespoon and your fingers, scoop and shape rounded spoonfuls of the beef mixture, forming balls and placing them on the broiler tray. When all the meatballs have been shaped, broil them close to the heat until golden brown, turning them over once (they'll flatten slightly)—about 5 minutes per side.

While the meatballs are broiling, start the sauce. In a large skillet or saucepan, heat the oil with the shallot and garlic over moderate heat. When they sizzle, add the tomatoes, breaking them up with your hands, and the remaining ingredients. Simmer the sauce until thick but still slightly liquid, about 10 minutes, adding the meatballs for the final few minutes of simmering.

Serve over cooked pasta.

Serves 4

Dietary information per serving (sauce only):
Calories: 286   *Cholesterol:* 54 mg
Fat: 14.4 g   *Sodium:* 171 mg

BEEFSTEAK STROGANOFF

Beef Stroganoff is usually considered one of the richest main courses you could eat. Here, it's transformed into a surprisingly light topping for pasta.

Serve over thin-to-medium strands, such as angel hair, spaghettini, spaghetti, linguine, tagliatelli, or fettuccine.

- **1 tablespoon corn oil**
- **2 medium shallots, chopped fine**
- **2 medium garlic cloves, chopped fine**
- **½ pound button mushrooms, cut into ¼-inch-thick slices**
- **1 cup evaporated nonfat milk**
- **½ pound well-trimmed top round steak, about 1 inch thick**
- **Freshly ground black pepper**
- **½ cup imitation sour cream**
- **1 tablespoon double-concentrate tomato paste**
- **1 teaspoon sugar**
- **2 tablespoons finely chopped fresh chives**
- **1 tablespoon finely chopped fresh Italian parsley**

Remove the broiler tray and spray it lightly with nonstick cooking spray. Preheat the broiler without the tray.

In a large skillet or saucepan, heat the oil with the shallots and garlic over moderate heat. When they sizzle, raise the heat to high and add the mushrooms. Sauté, stirring continuously, until the mushrooms begin to brown, 3 to 4 minutes. Add the evaporated milk and simmer until it is thick and reduced by about a third, 7 to 10 minutes.

While the milk is reducing, generously season both sides of the steak with pepper. Put the steak on the broiler tray and broil it close to the heat until it is well charred but still fairly rare inside, about 5 minutes per side. Cut the steak crosswise diagonally into ¼-inch-thick slices, saving the meat's juices; add the meat and its juices to the sauce and stir in the sour cream, tomato paste, and sugar.

Simmer briefly until heated through, then serve over cooked pasta. Garnish with chives and parsley.

Serves 4

Dietary information per serving (sauce only):
Calories: 284   *Cholesterol:* 35 mg
Fat: 16.2 g   *Sodium:* 183 mg

GRILLED BEEF FILLET WITH ROASTED PEPPER PESTO

There's a decidedly nouvelle flair to this presentation, in which slices of lean, grilled steak are draped atop a sweet-red-pepper sauce that has been spooned over a bed of pasta.

Serve over thin-to-medium strands, such as angel hair, spaghettini, spaghetti, linguine, tagliatelli, or fettuccine.

¾ pound well-trimmed top round steak, about 1
    inch thick
Freshly ground black pepper
4 medium red bell peppers, roasted, stemmed,
    peeled, and seeded (see page 10), juices saved
1 ounce grated Parmesan cheese
6 tablespoons lemon juice
2 tablespoons olive oil
2 teaspoons dried oregano
1½ tablespoons finely shredded fresh basil leaves

Remove the broiler tray and spray it lightly with nonstick cooking spray. Preheat the broiler without the tray.

Generously season both sides of the steak with pepper. Put the steak on the broiler tray and broil it close to the heat until it is well charred but still fairly rare inside, about 5 minutes per side.

While the steak is broiling, make the pesto. Put the peppers and their juices, the Parmesan, lemon juice, olive oil, and oregano in a food processor fitted with the metal blade. Pulse the ingredients until they are coarsely chopped, then scrape down the bowl and process until the mixture is smoothly pureed.

When the steak is done, cut it crosswise diagonally into ¼-inch-thick slices, saving the juices. Spoon the pesto over cooked pasta. Drape the steak slices on top and spoon the meat juices over the steak. Garnish with basil.

Serves 4

Dietary information per serving (sauce only):
Calories: 360   *Cholesterol:* 54 mg
Fat: 19.1 g   *Sodium:* 173 mg

GROUND VEAL WITH MUSHROOMS IN TOMATO CREAM

Veal has a sweet, mild flavor that goes well with mushrooms and a creamy tomato sauce seasoned with sweetly perfumed tarragon leaves. Unless your butcher can assure you that his or her ground veal is as lean as can be, buy a very lean cut of veal stew meat—a little more than the recipe calls for—and trim it by hand and chop it in your food processor.

Serve over fine-to-medium strands or ribbons.

　　1 tablespoon peanut or corn oil
　　3 medium shallots, chopped fine
　　6 ounces button mushrooms, cut into ¼-inch-thick slices
　　½ pound lean veal stewing meat, trimmed of all visible fat and chopped fine
　　1 16-ounce can salt-free whole tomatoes
　　½ cup evaporated nonfat milk
　1½ tablespoons double-concentrate tomato paste
　　2 teaspoons sugar
　　¾ teaspoon finely chopped fresh tarragon leaves
　　1 bay leaf

In a large saucepan or skillet, heat the oil with the shallots over moderate heat. When they sizzle, raise the heat to moderate-to-high, add the mushrooms, and sauté them for about 1 minute.

Add the veal and sauté it, stirring and breaking up the meat with a wooden spoon, until it loses its pink color, 3 to 5 minutes.

Add the tomatoes, breaking them up with your hands, and stir in the remaining ingredients. Simmer the sauce until it is thick but still slightly liquid, 20 to 25 minutes. Spoon over cooked pasta.

Serves 4

Dietary information per serving (sauce only):
Calories: 201   *Cholesterol:* 41 mg
Fat: 8.1 g   *Sodium:* 145 mg

VEAL-AND-ROSEMARY MEATBALLS WITH CHERRY TOMATOES

Rosemary is a natural companion to veal, and it delicately scents these fine-textured meatballs, served atop a rapid sauté of fresh cherry tomatoes.
Serve over fine-to-medium strands or ribbons.

VEAL-AND-ROSEMARY MEATBALLS

¾ pound lean veal stewing meat, trimmed of all
   visible fat and chopped fine
4 low-salt saltine crackers, finely crumbled
2 egg whites
1 medium shallot, chopped fine
¾ teaspoon dried rosemary
½ teaspoon freshly ground white pepper

SAUTEED CHERRY TOMATOES

2 tablespoons olive oil
2 medium garlic cloves, chopped fine
1½ pounds firm, ripe cherry tomatoes, stemmed and
   halved
2 tablespoons finely chopped fresh Italian parsley
2 tablespoons finely chopped fresh chives
1 teaspoon sugar

Put all the ingredients for the meatballs in a mixing bowl. With your hands, squeeze the ingredients together until thoroughly blended.

Remove the broiler tray and spray it lightly with nonstick cooking spray. Preheat the broiler without the tray.

With a tablespoon and your fingers, scoop and shape rounded spoonfuls of the veal mixture, forming balls and placing them on the broiler tray. When all the meatballs have been shaped, broil them close to the heat until golden brown, turning them over once (they'll flatten slightly)—about 5 minutes per side.

While the meatballs are broiling, sauté the cherry tomatoes. In a large skillet, heat the olive oil with the garlic over moderate heat. When the garlic sizzles, add the tomatoes and stir in the herbs and sugar. Simmer, stirring frequently, until the sauce is thick but still somewhat liquid, 5 to 7 minutes.

Spoon the tomatoes over cooked pasta. Place the meatballs on top.

Serves 4

Dietary information per serving (sauce only):
Calories: 255   *Cholesterol:* 60 mg
Fat: 14.4 g   *Sodium:* 104 mg

LAMB AND EGGPLANT WITH SPICED YOGURT

If you're already a convert to Middle Eastern cooking, the recipe title alone should tempt you. If you're not, suffice it to say that this dish tantalizes with a combination of voluptuous and spicy, yet mild and comforting, tastes. The eggplant, hoop cheese, and low-fat yogurt contribute to the richness while keeping the calories and fat down.

Serve over medium strands, ribbons, shells, or shapes.

> 10 ounces eggplant, peeled and cut into ¾- to 1-inch chunks
> 3 tablespoons lemon juice
> 2 tablespoons olive oil
> 2 medium garlic cloves, chopped fine
> 1 small onion (about 3 ounces), chopped fine
> ½ tablespoon grated fresh ginger root
> ¼ teaspoon ground cumin
> ¼ teaspoon ground turmeric
> ½ pound lean lamb stewing meat, trimmed of all visible fat and chopped fine
> 1 cup low-fat yogurt
> ¼ pound hoop cheese, at room temperature
> ¼ cup finely chopped fresh cilantro leaves

In a mixing bowl, toss the eggplant chunks with 1 tablespoon each of the oil and lemon juice. Leave to marinate for about 30 minutes.

Remove the broiler tray and spray it lightly with nonstick cooking spray. Preheat the broiler without the tray.

Arrange the eggplant on the broiler tray and broil it, turning the chunks frequently, until tender and golden brown, 10 to 15 minutes.

While the eggplant is broiling, prepare the lamb with yogurt. In a large skillet or saucepan, heat the remaining oil with the garlic and onion over moderate heat. When the vegetables sizzle, add the ginger, cumin, and turmeric and sauté about 30 seconds more. Then add the lamb and sauté until it loses its pink color and begins to turn brown, about 5 minutes. Add the yogurt and stir continuously until it is heated through.

Scatter the eggplant chunks on top of cooked pasta. Dot small clumps of hoop cheese among the eggplant pieces. Spoon the lamb-and-yogurt sauce on top. Garnish with cilantro and sprinkle with the remaining lemon juice.

Serves 4

Dietary information per serving (sauce only):
Calories: 249   *Cholesterol:* 37 mg
Fat: 15.9 g   *Sodium:* 88 mg

LAMB OREGANATO

Think of this as a lamb version of a classic Bolognese sauce. Your best bet for lean ground lamb is to buy the leanest lamb stewing meat you can find and trim it of all visible fat, then chop it in your food processor with the metal blade.

Serve over medium strands, ribbons, shells, or shapes.

1 tablespoon olive oil
2 medium garlic cloves, chopped fine
1 medium onion (about 5 ounces), coarsely chopped
½ pound lean lamb stewing meat, trimmed of all visible fat and chopped fine
¼ teaspoon freshly ground black pepper
½ cup Chianti or other dry red wine
1 16-ounce can salt-free whole tomatoes
2 tablespoons finely chopped fresh oregano leaves
1 tablespoon double-concentrate tomato paste
1 teaspoon sugar
1 bay leaf

In a large saucepan or skillet, heat the olive oil with the garlic and onion over moderate heat. When they sizzle, add the lamb, sprinkle it with the pepper, and sauté it, stirring and breaking up the meat with a wooden spoon, until it begins to brown, 5 to 7 minutes.

Add the wine and stir and scrape well to deglaze the pan. Add the tomatoes, breaking them up with your hands, and stir in the remaining ingredients.

Simmer the sauce until it is thick but still slightly liquid, 20 to 25 minutes. Spoon over cooked pasta.

Serves 4

Dietary information per serving (sauce only):
Calories: 209   *Cholesterol:* 33 mg
Fat: 11.2 g   *Sodium:* 89 mg

HAM AND BLACK-EYED PEAS IN BROTH

There's a simple, comforting quality to this dish that makes it perfect for chilly evenings. Serve it over medium-sized tubes, shells, or shapes, in shallow soup bowls.

1 tablespoon olive oil
1 medium garlic clove, chopped fine
1 small onion, chopped fine
¾ pound light-style ham, cut into ½-inch chunks
1½ cups reduced chicken broth (see page 6)
¾ cup rinsed and drained canned black-eyed peas
2 tablespoons finely chopped fresh chives
1 tablespoon finely chopped fresh Italian parsley

In a large saucepan, heat the oil with the garlic and onion over moderate heat. When they sizzle, add the ham and sauté just until it begins to brown, about 5 minutes.

Add the broth and the black-eyed peas and simmer just until the peas are heated through, about 3 minutes more. Stir in the chives and parsley and ladle over cooked pasta.

Serves 4

Dietary information per serving (sauce only):
Calories: 167   *Cholesterol:* 34 mg
Fat: 6.8 g   *Sodium:* 1,433 mg

DICED HAM WITH BITTER GREENS, SHALLOTS, AND TOMATOES

The sweet, strong flavor of ham is complemented in this tomato-based sauce by the bite of shredded bitter greens and the mild yet assertive taste of shallots. By choosing a lean, low-salt variety of ham from your deli case, you'll keep the recipe light without losing any of its character. Use mustard or collard greens—whichever is available fresh in your produce section.

Serve over medium-to-large ribbons, shells, or shapes.

- 1 tablespoon olive oil
- 3 medium shallots, chopped fine
- 1 garlic clove, chopped fine
- ½ pound light-style ham, cut into ½-inch chunks
- ½ cup reduced chicken broth (see page 6)
- 1 16-ounce can salt-free whole tomatoes
- 2 tablespoons finely chopped fresh Italian parsley
- 1 tablespoon double-concentrate tomato paste
- 1 teaspoon sugar
- 1 bay leaf
- ¼ pound mustard greens, stemmed and cut crosswise into ½-inch-wide strips

In a large skillet or saucepan, heat the oil with the shallots and garlic over moderate heat. When they sizzle, add the ham and sauté just until it begins to brown, about 5 minutes.

Add the chicken broth, stirring and scraping to deglaze the pan. Then add the tomatoes, breaking them up with your hands, and stir in the parsley, tomato paste, sugar, and bay leaf.

Simmer the sauce until it is thick but still fairly liquid, 20 to 25 minutes, stirring in the greens about 10 minutes before the sauce is done. Spoon over cooked pasta.

Serves 4

Dietary information per serving (sauce only):
Calories: 143   *Cholesterol:* 22 mg
Fat: 4.9 g   *Sodium:* 760 mg

SWEET-AND-SOUR GROUND PORK

A light pasta-sauce variation on the Chinese favorite. Your best bet for lean ground pork is to buy the leanest cut available at your butcher—such as meaty loin chops—trim off all visible fat, and chop it in your food processor.
Serve over medium strands, ribbons, shells, or shapes.

- 1 tablespoon peanut or corn oil
- 3 medium garlic cloves, chopped fine
- 1 small onion (about 3 ounces), coarsely chopped
- 1 small green bell pepper, stemmed, seeded, and cut into ¼- to ½-inch pieces
- ½ pound extralean ground pork
- 2 teaspoons grated fresh ginger root
- 1 cup pineapple juice
- 1 16-ounce can salt-free whole tomatoes
- 1½ tablespoons double-concentrate tomato paste
- 1 tablespoon sugar
- 1 tablespoon lemon juice
- 1 bay leaf
- 2 tablespoons finely chopped fresh cilantro leaves

In a large saucepan or skillet, heat the olive oil over moderate heat. Add the garlic, onion, and bell pepper and sauté until tender, about 3 minutes.

Add the pork with the ginger and sauté, stirring and breaking up the meat with a wooden spoon, until it loses its pink color and just begins to brown, 3 to 5 minutes.

Add the pineapple juice and stir and scrape well to deglaze the pan. Add the tomatoes, breaking them up with your hands, and stir in the remaining ingredients, except the cilantro.

Simmer the sauce until it is thick but still slightly liquid, 20 to 25 minutes. Spoon over cooked pasta and garnish with cilantro.

Serves 4

Dietary information per serving (sauce only):
Calories: 207   *Cholesterol:* 29 mg
Fat: 5.8 g   *Sodium:* 113 mg

4
DAIRY SAUCES

LIGHT CARBONARA

FARMER'S SPAGHETTI

PIZZAIOLA

HOOP CHEESE WITH CINNAMON, NUTMEG, AND HONEY

HOOP CHEESE WITH PARSLEY, CHIVES, AND PARMESAN

CHILE CON QUESO

LIGHT ALFREDO

CHEDDAR WITH CANADIAN BACON

SWISS FONDUE

LOW-FAT CHEESE MEDLEY

ROQUEFORT CREAM

LIGHT CARBONARA

This variation of the classic "charcoal maker's" pasta sauce pares down the calories, fat, cholesterol, and sodium by the use of low-fat cheeses and the excellent egg substitutes now available in the freezer cases of most supermarkets.

Serve in the traditional style, with spaghetti or with other thin-to-medium strands or ribbons.

2 **4-ounce cartons egg substitute, defrosted**
2 **ounces part-skim-milk, low-salt Swiss cheese, shredded**
1 **ounce grated Parmesan cheese**
2 **tablespoons finely chopped fresh chives**
1 **tablespoon finely chopped fresh Italian parsley**
1 **tablespoon unsalted margarine**
1 **medium shallot, chopped fine**
2 **ounces thinly sliced light-style ham, cut into ¼-by-1-inch strips**
Freshly ground black pepper

In a mixing bowl, stir together the egg substitute, cheeses, chives, and parsley. Set them aside.

In a large skillet or saucepan, melt the margarine over moderate heat. Add the shallot and ham and sauté until the shallot is translucent, 1 to 2 minutes.

Add cooked and drained pasta to the skillet and pour in the egg-and-cheese mixture. Toss continuously until the sauce thickens and coats the pasta, 2 to 3 minutes.

Serve immediately and season generously to taste with black pepper.

Serves 4

Dietary information per serving (sauce only):
Calories: 129   *Cholesterol:* 15 mg
Fat: 6.8 g   *Sodium:* 316 mg

FARMER'S SPAGHETTI

When I was a child, my mom and grandma used to make a luncheon dish they called by this name—basically a mixture of hoop cheese or farmer cheese garnished with whatever vegetables—chopped up or shredded—were around. Some thirty or more years later, this is my adaptation of that memory—a light pasta topping of low-fat cheese embellished with shredded vegetables. Feel free to vary the latter to your taste.

Serve, naturally enough, over spaghetti.

14 ounces hoop cheese, at room temperature
½ cup low-fat plain yogurt
1 ounce grated Parmesan cheese (approximately 5 tablespoons)
2 ounces carrot, coarsely shredded (approximately ½ loose cup)
2 ounces pickling cucumber, coarsely shredded
2 ounces red radishes, coarsely grated
¼ medium red bell pepper, coarsely grated
2 medium scallions, trimmed and cut lengthwise into 1- to 2-inch slivers
¼ cup coarsely chopped fresh Italian parsley
2 tablespoons chopped fresh chives

In a mixing bowl, toss all the ingredients thoroughly with cooked pasta. Serve immediately.

Serves 4

Dietary information per serving (sauce only):
Calories: 134   *Cholesterol:* 8 mg
Fat: 3.7g   *Sodium:* 126 mg

PIZZAIOLA

As the name suggests, this topping aims to approximate the flavors of a pizza—a tangy tomato-based sauce full of melted mozzarella cheese and Parmesan. Be sure to search your supermarket's dairy case for the lowest-fat, part-skim-milk mozzarella you can find.

Serve over medium ribbons, strands, shells, or shapes.

1 tablespoon olive oil
3 medium garlic cloves, chopped fine
1 small onion, chopped fine
1 16-ounce can salt-free whole tomatoes
1 tablespoon double-concentrate tomato paste
2 teaspoons sugar
2 teaspoons dried oregano
1 teaspoon dried basil
½ pound low-salt, part-skim-milk mozzarella, cut into ½-inch chunks
1 ounce grated Parmesan cheese
Freshly ground black pepper

In a large skillet or saucepan, heat the oil with the garlic and onion over moderate heat. When the vegetables sizzle, add the tomatoes, breaking them up with your hands. Stir in the tomato paste, sugar, oregano, and basil.

Simmer until the sauce is thick but still slightly liquid, 7 to 10 minutes. Stir in the cheeses and simmer briefly, just until the mozzarella is partially melted. Serve over cooked pasta and season to taste with black pepper.

Serves 4

Dietary information per serving (sauce only):
Calories: 255   *Cholesterol:* 35 mg
Fat: 13.3 g   *Sodium:* 546 mg

HOOP CHEESE WITH CINNAMON, NUTMEG, AND HONEY

I like to think of this as a light pasta version of cheese blintzes. And like blintzes, it makes an ideal brunch or luncheon dish when you fancy something a little bit sweet.

Serve over medium strands or ribbons, such as spaghetti, linguine, fettuccine, or fettuccelli.

14 **ounces hoop cheese, at room temperature**
¼ **cup evaporated nonfat milk**
¼ **cup honey, at room temperature**
1 **teaspoon powdered cinnamon**
⅛ **teaspoon grated nutmeg**

In a mixing bowl, stir and mash all the ingredients together until smoothly blended. Then toss thoroughly with just-cooked pasta and serve immediately.

Serves 4

Dietary information per serving (sauce only):
Calories: 259   *Cholesterol:* 2 mg
Fat: 1 g   *Sodium:* 28 mg

HOOP CHEESE WITH PARSLEY, CHIVES, AND PARMESAN

This simple, savory preparation is excellent as a light luncheon dish.
Serve over thin-to-medium strands or ribbons, such as angel hair, spaghettini, spaghetti, linguine, or fettuccine.

> 14 ounces hoop cheese, at room temperature
> ¼ cup evaporated nonfat milk
> 1 ounce grated Parmesan cheese
> ¼ cup finely chopped fresh Italian parsley
> ¼ cup finely chopped fresh chives

In a mixing bowl, stir and mash all the ingredients together until smoothly blended. Then toss thoroughly with just-cooked pasta and serve immediately.

Serves 4

Dietary information per serving (sauce only):
Calories: 116   *Cholesterol:* 7 mg
Fat: 2.8 g   *Sodium:* 116 mg

CHILE CON QUESO

In Mexico, the dish that goes by this name is served as an appetizer dip—a melt of cheeses seasoned with fresh jalapeño peppers. I've adapted it to a pasta sauce, taking advantage of the excellent light cheeses now available in most deli cases. (Be careful not to touch your eyes or other sensitive areas after handling the chile; wash your hands well.)

Serve over medium ribbons, such as tagliatelli or fettuccine.

- **1 tablespoon peanut or corn oil**
- **1 medium garlic clove, chopped fine**
- **½ small jalapeño pepper, seeded and chopped fine**
- **1 cup evaporated nonfat milk**
- **6 ounces low-salt, part-skim-milk cheddar cheese, shredded**
- **¼ pound low-salt, part-skim-milk Monterey Jack cheese, shredded**
- **2 tablespoons finely chopped fresh cilantro**

In a large saucepan, heat the oil with the garlic and jalapeño over moderate heat. When they sizzle, add the evaporated milk and, stirring frequently and taking care that the milk doesn't boil over, simmer briskly until it has reduced by about a third and has a creamy consistency, 7 to 10 minutes.

Reduce the heat slightly and gradually sprinkle and stir in the cheeses. Continue stirring until they have melted completely. Then spoon the sauce over cooked pasta and garnish with cilantro.

Serves 4

Dietary information per serving (sauce only):
Calories: 215   *Cholesterol:* 25 mg
Fat: 9.6 g   *Sodium:* 345 mg

LIGHT ALFREDO

The sauce made famous by Rome's Alfredo alla Scrofa restaurant is rich with butter, cream, and Parmesan cheese. By substituting nonfat evaporated milk for the first two of those ingredients, you get a delicious sauce that's far lighter in fat and calories—and incredibly simple to make.

Serve, in the traditional style, with fettuccine.

1 cup evaporated nonfat milk
¼ pound grated Parmesan cheese
Freshly ground black pepper

In a large saucepan, bring the evaporated milk to a simmer over moderate heat. Stir in the Parmesan and, as soon as it has melted and the sauce is thick and creamy, pour over cooked pasta. Season to taste with black pepper.

Serves 4

Dietary information per serving (sauce only):
Calories: 147   *Cholesterol:* 23 mg
Fat: 7.1 g   *Sodium:* 424 mg

CHEDDAR WITH CANADIAN BACON

A light variation on that old favorite, macaroni and cheese.
Serve over medium-sized tubes or shells.

- **1 tablespoon peanut or corn oil**
- **½ small onion, chopped fine**
- **2 ounces Canadian bacon, sliced thin and then cut into ¼-inch dice**
- **1 cup evaporated nonfat milk**
- **6 ounces low-salt, part-skim-milk cheddar cheese, shredded**
- **1½ tablespoons finely chopped, fresh Italian parsley**

In a large saucepan or skillet, heat the oil with the onion over moderate heat. When the onion sizzles, add the bacon and sauté, stirring continuously, for about 1 minute.

Add the evaporated milk to the pan and bring it to a simmer. Gradually stir in the cheese and continue simmering just until it has melted and the sauce is smooth and creamy. Pour over cooked pasta and garnish with parsley.

Serves 4

Dietary information per serving (sauce only):
Calories: 198   *Cholesterol:* 27 mg
Fat: 10.3 g   *Sodium:* 289 mg

SWISS FONDUE

The favorite Swiss-cheese dip for bread cubes is adapted here into a light but rich-tasting pasta sauce making the most of the low-salt, part-skim-milk Swiss cheeses now widely available.

Serve over medium strands or ribbons.

1 cup evaporated nonfat milk
1 medium garlic clove, chopped fine
½ pound low-salt, part-skim-milk Swiss cheese, shredded
1 tablespoon kirsch liqueur

In a large saucepan or skillet, bring the evaporated milk with the garlic to a simmer over moderate heat. Gradually stir in the cheese and, as soon as it has melted and the sauce is creamy, stir in the kirsch. Pour the sauce immediately over cooked pasta.

Serves 4

Dietary information per serving (sauce only):
Calories: 177   *Cholesterol:* 21 mg
Fat: 8.1 g   *Sodium:* 144 mg

LOW-FAT CHEESE MEDLEY

A cheese-lover's dream come true in a light pasta sauce! Feel free to vary the number and proportions of cheeses according to your taste and to what's available at your market.

Serve over medium strands, ribbons, shapes, or shells.

> 1 cup evaporated nonfat milk
> 2 ounces low-salt, part-skim-milk cheddar cheese, shredded
> 2 ounces low-salt, part-skim-milk Swiss cheese, shredded
> 2 ounces low-salt, part-skim-milk Monterey Jack cheese, shredded
> 1 ounce grated Parmesan cheese
> 1 tablespoon finely chopped fresh Italian parsley
> 1 tablespoon finely chopped fresh chives

In a large saucepan or skillet, bring the evaporated milk to a simmer over moderate heat. Gradually stir in the cheeses. As soon as they have melted and the sauce is creamy, pour over cooked pasta. Garnish with parsley and chives.

Serves 4

Dietary information per serving (sauce only):
Calories: 170
Fat: 7.9 g
Cholesterol: 26 mg
Sodium: 214 mg

ROQUEFORT CREAM

While Roquefort cheese is fairly high in fat and salt, a little of it goes a long way in this extraordinarily rich-tasting sauce.
Serve over medium strands or ribbons.

2¼ cups evaporated nonfat milk
1 medium garlic clove, whole
6 ounces Roquefort cheese, crumbled

In a large saucepan, bring the evaporated milk with the garlic to a boil over moderate heat. Simmer briskly until it has reduced by about a third, stirring frequently to prevent the milk from boiling over. Then sprinkle in the Roquefort, stirring just until it has melted. Pour over cooked pasta.

Serves 4

Dietary information per serving (sauce only):
Calories: 242   *Cholesterol:* 45 mg
Fat: 13.3 g   *Sodium:* 935 mg

INDEX